VOICES OFF

Talking About Schizophrenia

VOICES OFF

Talking About Schizophrenia

Georgia Brask

Cherish
EDITIONS

First published in Great Britain 2023 by Cherish Editions

Cherish Editions is a trading style of Shaw Callaghan Ltd & Shaw Callaghan 23 USA, INC.

The Foundation Centre

Navigation House, 48 Millgate, Newark

Nottinghamshire NG24 4TS UK

www.triggerhub.org

Text Copyright © 2023 Georgia Brask

All rights reserved. No part of this publication may be reproduced, stored in a retrieval system, or transmitted in any form or by any means, electronic, mechanical, photocopying, recording or otherwise, without prior permission in writing from the publisher

British Library Cataloguing in Publication Data

A CIP catalogue record for this book is available upon request from the British Library

ISBN: 978-1-913615-68-0

This book is also available in the following eBook formats:

ePUB: 978-1-913615-69-7

Georgia Brask has asserted her right under the Copyright, Design and Patents Act 1988 to be identified as the author of this work

Cover design by More Visual

Typeset by Lapiz Digital Services

Cover illustration by Georgia Brask

Illustrations by Georgia Brask

Cherish Editions encourages diversity and different viewpoints; however, all views, thoughts, and opinions expressed in this book are the author's own and are not necessarily representative of Cherish Editions as an organization.

All material in this book is set out in good faith for general guidance and no liability can be accepted for loss or expense incurred in following the information given. In particular, this book is not intended to replace expert medical or psychiatric advice. It is intended for informational purposes only and for your own personal use and guidance. It is not intended to diagnose, treat or act as a substitute for professional medical advice. The author is not a medical practitioner nor a counsellor, and professional advice should be sought if desired before embarking on any health-related programme.

TABLE OF CONTENTS

PROLOGUE

"Slow and steady wins the race."

Hearing voices is a horrible experience and, when you have 200 of them, it can be difficult to hear yourself above the din.

It took me a long time to find my voice – but I have – and this is what I would like to tell you.

ABOUT THE AUTHOR

My name is Georgia. I was born in 1994 and spent the first ten years of my life in London before my family (parents and younger brother) relocated to Denmark in 2005. My father is Danish, my mother Scottish and, as a lucky consequence of that, I am bilingual. In 2012, I was diagnosed with paranoid schizophrenia (PS). At that time in Denmark, there were no books about PS that were written from a personal perspective, so I found comfort and reassurance in reading English-language blogs. After much self-doubt and personal boundary-crossing, I started writing (on my Danish-language blog) about my experience and the repercussions of schizophrenia.

I needed to put things into words. Outside of my immediate family and closest friends, I struggled to speak – so writing became my outlet. Everything I couldn't say in real life, I could say in my blog, and it was really important to me that my message was accessible and understood. I wanted to be heard – but I also wanted to help.

The blog started from an overwhelming need to express myself, but it was to become something that was read by sufferers, carers and medical professionals. Schizophrenia, like many other mental illnesses, is highly misunderstood, and I was so happy that my words were helping people to understand it a little better. Unexpectedly, my blog was picked up by a Danish publisher, Muusmann Forlag, and the resulting book, *Georgias Stemme(r)*, reached the Danish bestseller list! Many people asked about the possibility of an English translation of my book, but, on reflection, I decided that I would rather do a complete rewrite for the English market – and that is the book that you are reading or listening to now.

My greatest wish is that I can help others who are struggling by sharing what I have learned about living with schizophrenia. Obviously, I'm not a medical professional and can't diagnose or treat anyone, but I can empathize, and I know from personal experience what it's like to live with severe mental illness. Schizophrenia is devastating and has the potential to ruin your life – but I would like to give hope to sufferers and the people who care for them. I am much more than my diagnosis and would love it if the information contained in these chapters could inspire, entertain and encourage people to try to bridge the gap between those considered "normal" and those considered… "weird".

Thank you – and happy reading!
Georgia

CHAPTER 1
THE BEGINNING

I'm three years old.

I've just woken up.

I'm looking at the painting on the wall opposite my bed.

I might have yawned; I don't remember all the details.

I do know, however, that this was the first time I became aware there was something in my head that was not my own thoughts.

It might even be my very first memory; maybe that's why it's lodged so firmly at the back of my head (behind all the song lyrics I cannot seem to forget and the black hole where names and faces go to disappear).

I can't remember what they said. I don't recall them being hostile, just intrusive – a blip on my regular frequency.

They were, as I would learn later, auditory hallucinations.

Voices.

The main symptom of schizophrenia is voices in your head – but, at three years old, how was I to know that?

I never told anyone.

I'm telling you now.

Welcome to my story.

CHAPTER 2
THE CHAOS

I was sectioned on yellow papers.

That's one of two ways one gets sectioned in Denmark, the other being red papers.

Red papers are for severely mentally ill patients, evaluated as being "a danger to themselves or others" (understood to be at risk of suicide or violent behaviour).

Yellow papers are for severely mentally ill patients whose doctors evaluate that the prospect of recovery (or a substantial improvement in their condition) will be significantly impaired if they are not hospitalized.

I was furious and didn't speak to my GP for a long time after that. Looking back, I understand that being committed to the ward ASAP was the right decision for me, but I was so angry about what felt like a deep violation of my freedom. However, it was definitely for the best because I was acutely psychotic and didn't know "whether it was Christmas or Tuesday", as my Scottish grandmother used to say!

I was hospitalized on 16 December 2011, following an extremely chaotic and distressing time for me and my family. In the months leading up to the hospitalization, everyone around me could see that there was something very "wrong" with me, but they didn't know what. Meanwhile, I didn't think there was anything wrong with me at all! I thought the problem was with everyone else, all whilst I was growing increasingly erratic, paranoid and withdrawn.

This is a common symptom of schizophrenia – lack of insight into one's own illness.

Despite hearing voices since I was three years old – something that my family were completely unaware of – it was only when I reached the age of 18 that I was diagnosed with paranoid schizophrenia. The average age for developing schizophrenia falls between late adolescence and early adulthood, with men tending to develop it earlier than women. This is a critical time in one's life because you're making the transition from teenager to adult with all the resulting responsibilities: moving away from home, making important education and career choices, deepening friendships and romantic relationships. Basically, it's a terrible time for illness to strike and shatter all your plans – but that's typically when it does.

Childhood schizophrenia is rare in comparison. On average, only 1 in 40,000 children are diagnosed with schizophrenia, compared to 1 in 100 adults. So, as someone who has heard voices my whole life, it feels weirdly "special" to be part of the childhood schizophrenia statistic!

I was finishing my first year of Danish high school (*gymnasium*) when my family started noticing changes in my behaviour: I was much quieter than normal, less interested in everything, less present. This gradually developed into completely nonsensical and baffling behaviour as the illness worsened. I would spend days lying on my bed, facing the wall, saying absolutely nothing – even when spoken to – seemingly paralysed and mute. On other occasions, I would make crazy demands of my parents, pacing back and forth like a lawyer in a bad movie, instructing them "how it is going to be from now on!" and demanding they did exactly as I commanded. During one particular episode, I forced my father to leave an important meeting, cancel all his business appointments for the rest of the day and drive home – only to tell him that the "emergency" was that he and my mother should buy me a car and a flat and get me a job – immediately!

Needless to say, they didn't. During a much darker episode, I locked myself in my bedroom with my blinds shut and wouldn't answer my mum when she repeatedly knocked on the door and asked if I was okay. After I didn't respond for some time, our neighbour had to break down my bedroom door, and he had no idea what awaited him. He found me sitting on my bed catatonic, uncomprehending, unable to speak and filled with inexpressible rage – and having pulled out all my eyebrows and eyelashes. Another time, I ran away from home on my brother's birthday, stayed out all night and didn't return until late the next day, at which point my parents had contacted the police. On two other occasions, I removed all the furniture and possessions from my bedroom – and I mean *eeeeeeeverything* – and put them in a big pile in the garden after covering them in a sparse web of cling film to protect them from the Danish rain. (Have you ever tried to cling film a chest of drawers?) I think my logic at the time was that I didn't want any of it cluttering up my room and my mind. I needed a completely clear and empty space to try to find some kind of control over things. I didn't want to be me. I suspect that I ran away from home because I found people overwhelming; I needed to get away from everything and everyone without really understanding what was going on in my own head that would merit such a reaction. I needed to stop the noise and find a safe place away from the voices and the chaos in my head. And so, the bizarre behaviour continued...

When I was committed to the youth psychiatric ward, my parents were advised not to visit me for the first two weeks because I required "total and absolute peace" to let my frazzled brain rest and restart. After that, they would come to see me daily, sometimes twice a day. Initially, the meetings were just a few minutes because I was so restless and could only tolerate extremely brief moments with people. I barely spoke and eye contact was non-existent but, over time, my tolerance level increased, and the visits became longer. I would remain in hospital for seven months.

The first three months were spent in the closed unit, away from all the other patients. This was not because I was a danger to others, but because I needed to give my brain time to recover in a peaceful environment without too much input. As I would later learn, daily impressions "go right in" when you have schizophrenia. Put simply, this is due to a broken filter system in the schizophrenic brain. Healthy people have a well-functioning filter system, which keeps out all the stuff that doesn't matter (in the same way that your eyes can always see your nose, but your filter system/brain tells them to ignore it). However, with schizophrenia, that filter system is defective, meaning you get bombarded by ALL the impressions you experience – and that is exhausting.

I remember one of the first weekends I spent at the ward. My mum came to visit in the evening, and we decided that we would watch *The X Factor*. We had the ward to ourselves – the other patients had all gone home – and we had sweets and popcorn at the ready. We had just made ourselves comfortable when, after five minutes, I had to go to bed because I was so overwhelmed and could not keep watching the TV. My poor mum had to pack everything up and drive home again – and she didn't even like *The X Factor*!

The above example illustrates that, in the early days of my recovery, simply watching television was too much for me, *waaaaaaaaaay* too much input for a shattered brain to cope with. I've always been sensitive, but that stunned me; just five minutes of watching television was intolerable. At the time, it made me feel vulnerable, small and fragile. I mean, what kind of weakling gets exhausted just from watching a light-hearted television show?

It was one of the first times I became aware of the early ramifications of my illness.

There's a popular way of describing the connection between stress, sensitivity and mental illness known as the Stress-Vulnerability Model.

The model shows that, while one person can be exposed to a significant amount of stress before they develop a mental illness, another person's stress threshold can be considerably lower. In any case, whether you become mentally ill depends both on how you TOLERATE stress and how many stressful events you EXPERIENCE in your life. If a person has a propensity toward psychosis, it is the balance between those two components that can make a huge difference.

CHAPTER 3
TRUE TO MYSELF

If you could write a letter to your teenage self, what would you say?

"Don't worry!"

"Just be yourself!"

"Things get better!"

None of the above?

If I could tell 14-year-old me anything, it wouldn't be *any* of the above. "Don't worry" wouldn't have any effect (I'm a natural over-thinker and would just get annoyed); "just be yourself" would frustrate me, too (that's exactly what I was doing already, and it only seemed to be exacerbating the problem); and as for "things get better"… er, not if "get better" means a psychotic breakdown in the future.

The most honest thing I could tell my 14-year-old self is, "Never, as in never-ever, stop being 100% true to yourself." It requires inner strength, determination and confidence – not easy if you suffer from mental illness – but I've learned the hard way that putting aside your own truth to try to fit in or be what you think others expect of you will only make you feel worse in the long run. If I could speak to my younger self, I would stress the importance of being your authentic self, no matter how scary it feels.

However, 14-year-old Georgia's biggest problem made it difficult to "be true to herself" because 14-year-old Georgia's biggest problem was... bullies.

When I was ten years old, my family and I moved from London to Roskilde, a mid-sized town in Denmark. I had no problem with the move itself, viewing it as a kind of adventure, but problems began to arise during the years I was in Danish primary school (*folkeskole*).

First off, because I was bright, I was placed in the class above, meaning that I was a year younger than everyone else. So, when the other girls hit puberty and began discussing clothes, make-up and guys, I was still a little girl collecting soft toys and Pokémon games. However, in retrospect, this was the easiest (ha, ha... *heavy* sarcasm) time I had at Danish school because, as I became a teenager, things just got worse.

It started with the other kids teasing me about my accent and the way I pronounced things. I quickly learned Danish spelling and grammar, but my pronunciation lagged despite having spoken Danish at home all my life. My classmates picked on this. I tried to ignore it – and that's when they started throwing water bottles at my head.

It didn't stop there. They would take my water bottle and poke holes in it, drink from it or even throw it around the classroom while I struggled to get it back. They would pull my hair so hard I screamed, and repeatedly pinch my tummy shouting "fatty!" until I broke down crying in a lesson, which, in turn, prompted them to scream "cry baby!" They would giggle and whisper when I said something in class and try to push me off my bike when I was cycling home. They would leave what appeared to be nice comments on my Facebook photos, only to follow up with, "Just kidding!" And, at the Year 9 farewell party – the last time we'd see each other as a class before going on to the next stages of our education – I was told that I was "useless, boring and no one would ever want me".

Needless to say, I was glad to see the back of them.

I wish I could say that most of this happened when there were no adults (i.e. teachers) around to witness it – but that was not the case. Perhaps if the so-called "strong anti-bullying policies" most schools claim to have *actually* existed, it wouldn't have got that far… but it did, and that's why I'm writing about it now. My experience of the Danish school system would suggest that one of the requirements for being a teacher is an ability to turn a blind eye to bullying in all its shapes and forms.

Some may say that being bullied so badly is somehow a good thing – that it has toughened me up and made me stronger. I beg to differ. I'm still sensitive and, as far as I am concerned, I was as strong as I needed to be *waaaaay* before I entered the Danish education system. Bullying doesn't make you stronger – all it does is take away valuable opportunities for someone to socialize and grow as a person. Try developing your conversational skills when you're systematically being excluded from everything by your classmates and peers!

As most bullying victims know, the damage your confidence suffers when you're constantly told "you're not good enough" or "you're not one of us" makes you believe it's your fault. The subject of bullying was never discussed by the school staff, and I had no wish to bring it up at home – so, I never told anyone what I was going through. My parents were aware I was being picked on a bit, but they didn't know the full extent of it. Now, with the knowledge and hindsight, they feel terrible that they were not aware of the hell that I was going through. I would like to see anti-bullying education as a compulsory subject in every school's curriculum and, when there is conflict, the school should address the issue immediately, suspend the bullies and make the parents aware of their child's bullying behaviour. I guess I don't belong to the group who believe you should turn the other cheek, no matter how many people preach it. Lily Allen had the right idea in her music video for "Smile" (check it out)… and that's all I'll say about that.

CHAPTER 4
HOW CAN I HELP YOU?

Stress and trauma cannot cause mental illness, but they can trigger it in someone who is predisposed to mental illness. My psychiatrist told my parents, "This was a path Georgia was going to go down regardless," meaning that I would have ended up experiencing psychosis sooner or later, but perhaps being bullied sped up the process.

Since childhood, I've always wanted to be an author. I never imagined my first book would become a reality because of a psychotic breakdown – it's a far cry from the stories about magical girls and talking animals I loved to write when I was little – but here we are. Being bullied has not toughened me up or benefited me in any way, and this book will not provide you with such outmoded clichés. Instead, I hope I can provide you with information, advice, familiarity and, most of all, hope.

I have written my story to help others in the same situation. It's also been an incredibly therapeutic process for me to share my experiences – so, for me, it's a win-win scenario if you get something from my words. Within the chapters of this book, I talk about my experiences with the illness, sharing tips, insights and things I've learned along the way. I have covered many topics related to schizophrenia that I hope will be relevant to you. If you have any questions, I have added my email at the end of the book (see Social Media – page 169); however, please note that I may take a while to get back to you. Though I will do my best to answer as thoroughly as I can, the nature of schizophrenia can make it difficult to communicate, and I am often easily overwhelmed. I do hope that you enjoy this book, and it would make me happy if you let me know what you think, whether via email or by leaving a book review. (Thank you!)

Between the chapters, I have included "Reality Checks", situations as perceived vs. how they actually are for me; "Quick Questions", based on ones I've been asked by friends and family that I hope will be of interest to you; and "Coping Strategies" that I've found useful in dealing with certain aspects of schizophrenia. Finally, I have illustrated the book, which I hope provides a little bit of fun and lifts what might otherwise be considered a dark and heavy subject.

Ultimately, I hope to show that schizophrenia isn't all doom and gloom or a disease that only creates seriously disturbed individuals – but that there are many ordinary young people like me, struggling with unimaginable challenges, who don't necessarily look like we're mentally ill. Schizophrenia is devastating, and the unfairness of it being a largely invisible illness just adds to the difficulties we face. Surely, if you *look* perfectly fine and act normally, then you must *be* fine, right?

Wrong.

This is an important point to make – just because I'm able to look after myself and dress nicely, and my outward appearance is in order, doesn't necessarily mean I'm able to function completely on par with everyone else. There are many things that challenge me daily – things that a "normal" person wouldn't give a second thought to: going into a busy supermarket or being stopped on the street by a charity collector. Just two examples of everyday life that can prove to be insurmountable hurdles for someone suffering with psychosis. This is particularly important to emphasize when faced with a job and education system that may or may not understand just how much schizophrenia – or mental illness in general – affects a person's life and capabilities. But more on that later…

Anyway, I won't keep you any longer. Read on for the next instalment in my story – and I hope you enjoy the journey.

REALITY CHECK

WHAT YOU SEE:

A young woman is sitting opposite her friend in a café, staring into her phone. She avoids eye contact with the waiter and doesn't seem to be engaged in anything around her.

WHAT'S ACTUALLY HAPPENING:

I'm looking at my Notes app, in which I've written down conversation topics and questions before meeting with my friend so that I will have interesting things to say and questions to ask her. So, what may look like rudeness to an observer is actually me doing my best to be prepared and re-activate my brain when I go blank in conversation. I find eye contact difficult and hope if I don't look at anyone, that will prevent them from approaching or striking up conversation with me. (I'm not unfriendly, just scared to mess up my words.)

CHAPTER 5
VOICES

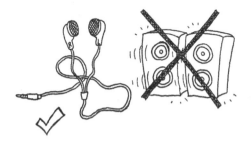

This chapter is dedicated to what I see as the worst symptom
of schizophrenia.

Yep, I'm talking about the voices.

I can split my voices into two groups: 24/7 and situation-based.
When I was at my most ill (around the time I was hospitalized and
for a while after I was discharged), I had 24/7 voices that were in my
head from the moment that I woke up to when I went to bed – no
breaks, no peace, no escape. A constant torrent of aggressive, loud,
nasty comments directed at me, or about me. "You're so stupid!"
"She's disgusting!" "What a loser!" "Shut up!" "We think you're
worthless!"

At that time, I had over 200 voices. Often, several of them would
be talking at the same time; some mumbling, some whispering, some
shouting. Although some were "neutral", meaning they didn't sound
like anyone in particular, many were voices of people I knew. Men's
voices. Women's voices. English voices. Danish voices. And they
just never stopped. They would regularly repeat the same things

over and over again: "You're weird. Weird. Weird. Weird. You're so weird. Weird. You're weird." Sometimes, when I was alone, I would tell them – out loud – "Shut up!" and they'd disappear for a while. When in company, I could make them go away momentarily by doing something discreet like shifting slightly in my seat or blinking, but no matter what I did, they always came back. They would pass judgment on my actions and tell me what to do, often in a threatening manner: "Don't eat those potatoes. You'll get sick!" "Don't you dare say that; they'll laugh at you!" Nothing was safe or hidden from them – not my actions, not my words, not even my own thoughts. I tried listening to music to block them out, but they would just shout louder. Eventually, I became dispirited. I broke down crying while on holiday with my family; it was a day when the voices had really been going at me, telling me that nobody liked me and how my friends were going to dump me because I was so boring. Deep down, I knew it wasn't true, but the voices were so convincing and told me this kind of thing all the time, sometimes in my friends' voices, so it was hard not to be affected by it. "Boring" echoed in my head afterwards; what if my friends really thought that? It hit me so hard. I felt like I'd reached breaking point that day, but I couldn't do anything other than cry out my frustration (after having a talk with my family about what the voices were saying), and then try to ignore the voices as best I could with my family's support.

It's strange because when I was very young, my voices were nice. It was only when I grew older that they became nasty. At their peak, I couldn't do anything other than lie in bed staring at a wall, my mind bombarded with horrible taunts and messages that I had no control over. For this reason, I am forever grateful that modern medicine can remove voices. Nowadays, I only hear my other type of voices: the situation-based ones, which arise due to external stress factors like going shopping or not getting enough sleep. I still experience voices daily, but the non-stop stream of verbal abuse is gone, thanks to my medicine, and the comments are of a neutral or positive nature.

The situation in which I am most likely to hear voices is during or after a social event – especially one that gives me a buzz. What the voices say is mostly based around my performance (i.e. whether

I'm doing well or not, or simply commenting on how I look or what I'm wearing). For example, "She's wearing a red T-shirt today," "You're doing well," "She looks tired," "They think she's cool." These voices can be irritating, but nowhere near as distressing as the 24/7 voices that I used to endure. In any case, I know that if the general tone starts getting negative again, it's a sign that I need to stop whatever I'm doing and slow right down. In a way, the voices are a kind of alarm system for my well-being, and I use them as a warning sign that things might be getting too stressful for me. It's a vicious cycle – on the one hand, my voices stress me, but on the other, they're my indicator of stress.

I know that a lot of sufferers have voices that tell them to harm themselves or other people. I feel fortunate to never have had that kind of dialogue. I've had voices that implied I *shouldn't* do something harmful, but in an encouraging way: "Don't pull that plastic bag over your head." "Imagine if you cut yourself on that knife." "If you drank that detergent, it would be terrible."

Of course, these voices were horrible because, even though they weren't directly telling me to do those things, I found it extremely uncomfortable that such morbid ideas were in my head. I should make it clear at this point that I've never been suicidal. Even in my darkest moments, I have not lost the will to live – and perhaps that's why the very negative voices were particularly scary for me. However, the 24/7 voices remain the worst for me – and I am very glad that the medicine has got them to shut up!

Many people ask how I hear my voices. The answer is, I don't hear them as if there was an actual person talking to me; I hear them coming from inside my own head, like my thoughts. The best way I can describe it is that they sound the way music sounds through earphones, rather than loudspeakers. When you listen to music through loudspeakers, there's a distance between you and the music – it's separate from you. When you listen through earphones, the music fills your head, and that's what it's like with my voices. However, every voice-hearer's experience is unique, so someone else might hear theirs in a different way. I hope this makes sense.

What kind of voices do you get? How do you cope with them?

CHAPTER 6
DISPROVING MYTHS

Well done, dear reader, you've reached this far, so here's a little gift for you to open:

Schizophrenia has nothing to do with multiple personalities.

Repeat after me:

Schizophrenia.
Has.
NOTHING.
To.
Do.
With.
Multiple.
Personalities.

Multiple personality disorder is a completely different illness (and is actually called dissociative identity disorder).

Now that you know this, you can tell everyone you know, right? Spread the word!

This chapter is about MYTHS.

I've just covered **Myth #1**, so let's go straight to the next one…

Myth #2: Schizophrenics are violent and dangerous.

Despite a generally uninformed and sensationalist media that insists on portraying all schizophrenics as "psycho killers", violence is not a symptom of schizophrenia. Unfortunately, it is the most tragic cases that make the headlines, but the vast majority of us are perfectly ordinary, peaceful people who just want to live our lives even though our symptoms make it incredibly challenging. In other words, we are NOT planning on going out and committing murder or stabbing you in your shower. This is an extremely unfair portrayal of an already vulnerable group of people who have enough to deal with as it is – we really don't need this extra stigma.

If you are by nature a violent person, it is possible that you might be a violent schizophrenic (or nurse, or car mechanic, or shop assistant, or actor, or…), but if you're not, you won't be. It's really that simple. A diagnosis of schizophrenia does not include a propensity toward violence – it is not a symptom. So, please, let's stop spreading that myth once and for all.

Myth #3: Schizophrenics belong in a mental hospital.

I've had my fair share of what my family call "tinfoil-hat moments" – our family survives on perseverance and humour – but do I belong in the psychiatric ward for the rest of my life? No. Nobody does. In fact, people with schizophrenia can lead productive, fulfilling lives after their diagnoses. I think the most important thing is to be realistic about what you can and cannot do and try to shape your life accordingly.

To illustrate: when I was discharged from hospital, I was transferred to outpatient care at District Psychiatry and would remain in their care for the following eight years. I was advised to go back to school, so I did. After the summer, I started a single-subject course at an adult education centre. My curriculum needed to be single-subject (as opposed to a full, five-day-a-week education) because that was as much as I could cope with. However, even two subjects a week proved too much. My voices got worse – I couldn't concentrate in class. Being with strangers was too overwhelming, and doing homework was like trying to climb Mount Everest. I felt that way because my cognitive symptoms, which I will describe in the following chapter, made it impossible to focus or understand the material. Unfortunately, I had to quit shortly after I'd started – and was never able to return to the Danish education system.

Holding down a job proved to be too much, as well. I got a part-time job at a family friend's publishing house – she was well-informed about my situation beforehand and had tailored the job accordingly. But I just couldn't live up to the expectations of the modern labour market. Tasks that are simple to others just weren't simple to me and, no matter how many measures my boss and colleagues took to accommodate my difficulties, I still found the requirements of the job too complicated and stressful to handle. Then, I had a relapse and had to stay at home for six months. We eventually agreed there was no future in the job for me, and, sadly, I had to resign.

Recovery is a long, slow process, easily disrupted by too much stress. It's important to start small – baby steps. "Take things one day at a time," as the nurses at the psychiatric ward instilled in us. Perhaps the kind of goals we should aim to achieve initially are things like taking our medicine every day, maintaining our personal hygiene routines, completing chores, being on time for appointments and so on – in other words, all the things that go out the window when you're in the throes of psychosis. If you can regain the ability to achieve all these "little" things, then you're doing great. In my experience, I found a regular job or study schedule too overwhelming – more about that later – which very negatively affected my ability to get basic, everyday tasks done. I've learned that, for me, focusing energy in one area of life means I have little left for another, so it is very important to manage my personal resources wisely to avoid relapse.

What I'm trying to say is this: most schizophrenics don't "belong in the mental hospital" – it is a temporary solution to a long-term situation. However, the many challenges of everyday life can be completely overwhelming, so it's important not to push oneself too far, either. Pace yourself, learn to say "no" and, above all, don't give up hope – you may just need to find a different path in life than the one on which you originally embarked.

Myth #4: Schizophrenia is caused by a bad upbringing.

I don't even know where to start with this one because, wow… nothing could be further from the truth. I had an amazing childhood with an abundance of happy memories, and my parents are the most switched-on, attentive, supportive and caring people I know. I would be furious if someone suggested they hadn't done their job properly! Let's just rule this one out right away, shall we?

Schizophrenia is caused by a mix of genetic, physical, psychological and environmental factors. It's not just one thing – several elements must be in place for someone predisposed to the illness to develop it, as I highlighted with the Stress-Vulnerability Model described in Chapter Two.

The myth that schizophrenia is caused by "a bad upbringing" is seriously outdated – I hope no psychiatrists or others working in healthcare actually believe it. However, there is no doubt that a strong, supportive family is a major contributor to *aiding* a successful recovery.

Myth #5: Schizophrenia is rare.

Statistically, 1 in 100 people will develop schizophrenia in their lifetime. So, if you have 99 friends, and none of them have it, maybe you – *gulp* – should start making your tinfoil hat. I know the tinfoil hat thing is probably not the most "woke" joke to make, but in my family, honest dialogue sprinkled with a little dark humour has been our saving grace. We have all earned the right to laugh in the face of schizophrenia every now and then!

You will almost certainly know at least one person who has it (and if you're in any doubt about whether you have it yourself, go and see your doctor). Schizophrenics aren't some mysterious, strange group of beings who emerge from asylums only when the nurses have forgotten to lock the gate – start rattling those chains. Schizophrenics live in the community and can function perfectly well outside of hospital. They could be the quiet guy in your maths class who finds it hard to make eye contact, the girl shifting nervously in her seat in the doctor's waiting room, or that woman you've noticed for her "unique" personal style in your local supermarket.

"Everyone you meet is fighting a battle you know nothing about. Be kind. Always." I feel this quote is highly relevant. As long as you are kind and genuinely concerned about the well-being of others, that's all one could ask for – especially when it comes to anyone struggling with mental illness who might require a little more kindness, patience and care than most. Now that you know every 100th person you meet could have schizophrenia, I hope you'll consider this when going about your day. Take a moment to understand that some people are struggling – they just might not look like they are.

CHAPTER 7
INVISIBLE ILLNESS

I'd never struggled academically. My hurdles had always been of a social nature. So, when I suddenly couldn't understand the maths problem I was reading, or when the teacher's instructions didn't "go in", I wonder, why didn't I tell anyone? Perhaps I didn't want to admit to my classmates I was falling behind. They'd have reached question four in our textbooks while I was still trying to make sense of question one, and I worried they'd think I was stupid if I asked, "What did the teacher say?" just minutes after she'd given us clear instructions.

Nonetheless, I sat there panicking, reading the task again and again, only to give up and copy someone else's notes. I simply couldn't absorb the information I was reading at all – and my classmates' apparent ease at understanding the work stressed me further. "Why can't I do this anymore? This should be simple for me!"

I would later learn that there was a term for this ailment: cognitive symptoms.

Just as heart disease is a heart disease, and kidney disease is a kidney disease, schizophrenia is a brain disease. It's not "just" a mental disorder that's "all in your head" – neither are any other forms of mental illness. It is a fundamental fault in the way the brain is programmed. Like other brain diseases, such as Alzheimer's and epilepsy, it creates concrete symptoms that affect one's functioning and performance in everyday life.

Some of these symptoms are invisible to an onlooker.

Schizophrenia in itself is an invisible illness. Unless you are actively psychotic and behaving irrationally, people cannot tell that you have it. This is one of the many cruel aspects of the disease. If you have a broken leg, people see your cast and crutches and sympathize accordingly – but you don't get given a walking stick for a broken brain. Mental illness isn't always transparent. Combined with the many myths, misunderstandings and taboos that surround schizophrenia, it's no wonder so many sufferers choose to keep quiet about their diagnosis. I did, too. For a long time. However, when I chose to open up about my experiences, it was a great relief.

I'd like to explain a little bit about some of the invisible aspects of schizophrenia:

Firstly, there are the cognitive symptoms – one of the lesser-known, yet highly disabling by-products of schizophrenia. When you have schizophrenia, you may experience difficulties with what's known as executive function: cognitive processes such as paying attention, concentrating, remembering things, planning ahead, following instructions, carrying out tasks and generally integrating your thoughts, feelings and behaviour. This can make many aspects of everyday life incredibly challenging. I can mention three examples that spring to mind from my own life:

Household chores

Let's face it, most people find them boring and tend to put them off until the last minute. However, when you have schizophrenia, there's more to it than simply disliking doing them. I actually don't mind cleaning and tidying when I feel able to, and would go so far to say that carrying out and completing these tasks gives me a sense of accomplishment. It's not so much a case of me being a lazy slob as it is a problem with low motivation. Believe it or not, it is a symptom of schizophrenia called avolition. Avolition can be defined as a lack of motivation or ability to carry out tasks or activities that have an end goal, such as paying bills or attending a family party. It often occurs in schizophrenia, but is also seen in depression and bipolar disorder.

When you clean, there are surprisingly many steps involved – steps that can tax motivation. Take hoovering, for example: first, you must go and get the hoover. Then, you bring it to the room you're intending to clean. Plug the hoover in. Switch it on. You have to move everything off the floor and place it on surfaces in your room so that you have as clear a space as possible to hoover. (This is five steps already – five steps that can easily tire out a fragile schizophrenic brain.) Then, you start hoovering, which isn't the most strenuous task in itself, but all too easy to lose interest in if your brain is disordered and overwhelmed already. You have to keep at it, staying focused while navigating around your room(s), making sure you stretch to reach the far corners and remember to go under your bed and furniture. You have to keep track of where you've hoovered, keep control of the nozzle at all times, try not to accidentally hoover any small possessions you may have laying around, and continue moving the hoover along the floor as you go, so it doesn't get stuck behind your desk or sofa. This may not sound like much, but when your brain isn't good at dealing with the unexpected and finds it overwhelming to maintain focus the more obstacles it encounters, something simple like hoovering can quickly drain energy reserves. The same goes for cleaning, where you have the added obstacles of paranoia about cleaning products – "What if the fumes from the loo bleach are dangerous mixed with the fumes from the glass cleaner?" – and you sometimes have to scrub quite hard to remove water stains. (I don't know if this occurs for other schizophrenics, but I find that I can't keep up strength exertion for long before feeling overwhelmed.) I know that, for someone with a "normally" wired brain, this probably sounds ridiculous, but even something as mundane as housework can be a huge challenge for the psychotic brain. I am quite good at it now… but it takes time, preparation and the ability to convince yourself that the scouring cream is not out to kill you!

I hope this helps anyone who is beating themselves up for not being able to follow through on simple tasks – you aren't alone.

Conversation

I'm sure that many introverts can relate to this one! A conversation isn't just opening your mouth and making sounds at someone. You must think on your feet, ask questions, read social cues, allow the other person to speak, contribute yourself, constantly assess if you should keep talking or politely excuse yourself, listen, comprehend, respond, repeat… and don't get me started on additional distractors such as loud music, alcohol and people dancing (e.g. at a nightclub).

When it comes to schizophrenia, the illness can make the ability to talk seem so insurmountable that it is avoided altogether. This can give people the impression you don't want to chat or socialize, no matter how false this may be. I have been labelled a "quiet girl", and people think I'm an introvert, when, in fact, I am quite social by nature and believe that, without my illness, I would have been much more outgoing.

Holding down a job

It's probably evident by now that when even very small things like chores and basic conversation are so overwhelming, being in a proper working environment is rather difficult. I was employed for a while but had to stop working when it became evident that I couldn't cope with the requirements of the job, which were realistic and normal. Being part of the modern labour market requires – as a minimum – an ability to follow instructions, planning skills, efficiency, the ability to communicate well and a certain amount of independence, none of which I could deliver, no matter how much I longed to be a useful and valued member of the team.

CHAPTER 8
THE TALKING BOOKSHELF

I'm eight.

The voices are still there, but now they're coming from places other than inside my head. When the water runs into the bath, I hear an aggressive whispering coming from the taps; when I use my hairdryer, there's a strange buzz of words I can't quite make out; when I brush my teeth with my electric toothbrush, I hear hostile-sounding noises that I interpret as words, but still cannot fully decipher.

Frightening stuff.

And still, I didn't tell anyone.

Not even about the bookshelf.

I had a bookshelf in my London bedroom. To this day, I don't know why, but at night, it would come alive with voices. Again – like the taps, hairdryer and toothbrush – they were incoherent, there were many of them, and none of them were friendly. I would hide under my duvet to block them out. How I managed to fall asleep every night, I don't know. Don't ask me why I didn't think to tell my parents, either – not even in passing. I just never did.

I sometimes wonder what my life would have been like if I'd been diagnosed with schizophrenia at an earlier age, but I'll never know.

What I do know is that I'm happy my books don't talk to me anymore – although I do hope this one talks to you, dear reader.

REALITY CHECK

WHAT YOU SEE:

I don't initiate conversation at the family gathering; instead, I'm sitting alone, staring into space and looking disinterested.

WHAT'S ACTUALLY HAPPENING:

I've zoned out due to being overwhelmed by too many impressions, and my brain has, in effect, switched off. My facial expression is blank, another symptom of schizophrenia called flat effect, where one's face is left devoid of expression.

In the early stages of my recovery, I found it impossible to speak at family gatherings. This didn't mean that I wasn't interested or comfortable within my family; I just found it too difficult to think of things to say – my voices commenting on everything I was doing didn't help – and my brain would shut down in the company of larger groups of people.

My mother, recognizing what was happening, would try to bring me back by asking me something mundane like, "Georgia, would you pass me the water jug, please?" That would snap my brain back on again and get me reconnected with my environment. Nowadays, I am more able to make conversation as long as I am within the bounds of a trusted group of people. Successful medical and psychiatric treatment, combined with the endless patience and understanding of my family, have played a large part in my ability to communicate better than ever before with my loved ones.

CHAPTER 9
PARANOIA

When you hear the word "paranoia", what comes to mind? A feeling of being watched? The television talking to you? Obsessive jealousy? Tinfoil hats?

In schizophrenia, paranoia can be described as thinking and feeling like you are being threatened in some way, even if there is little or no evidence that you are. Most people probably associate paranoia with the stereotypical portrayal of someone who believes that the government is spying on them, or that their mind is being controlled by aliens, or that they are the embodiment of Jesus.

In my case, paranoia is more subtle and nuanced. I've never had weird thoughts about the government or aliens, nor believed I was anyone other than myself (but I'm not dismissing that, for some people, these beliefs are present, scary and very real). I've just never experienced them.

For me, paranoia could manifest itself as issues about food – "best before" dates were/are a minefield for me, and I am truly terrified by the possibility of food poisoning. In the past, I would obsessively check the dates on food packets and often asked my mum, "Okay, I'm just being paranoid, but are the spareribs supposed to be this colour?" or "Are baked beans okay to eat two days after the expiry date?" Sometimes, I couldn't bring myself to finish the food on my plate because I was so scared that I was going to get food poisoning. "Don't eat those potatoes. You'll get sick!" the voices would say. They put thoughts in my head that I would begin to dread. I am phobic about throwing up, especially the preliminary nausea part where you know it's going to happen, but you can't do anything to stop it. So, my voices were extremely effective in preventing me from eating certain parts of my meal if I didn't manage to fight through them. At one stage, I would panic about eating anything that was naturally green coloured – so, spinach was definitely out! My long-suffering mum would assure me that she had absolutely no intention of poisoning me or any member of our family.

I am still pathologically terrified of being sick, so much so that I will shake uncontrollably and become tearful if my stomach so much as gurgles. My mum often has to remind me, "If your stomach is rumbling, it's because you are hungry, not because you're going to throw up, so don't panic." Nowadays, I understand that paranoia has played a big part in creating this fear and I can usually talk myself down from it. To be honest, though, since the medicine started working and my psychosis has abated, I am much better than I was. I am now able to eat and not really think about it (or, at least, I push my thoughts aside). Occasionally, I will ask a food-date or preparation question, but I will acknowledge that I'm being paranoid and, as my mum often retorts, why would she serve me anything that she had the slightest doubt about? I've never had an eating disorder and can generally eat anything I want in moderation, so it's a shame that my paranoia, and the accompanying voices, have had this influence on my otherwise completely healthy eating habits.

My mum says that, when I was very ill and when I had my relapse, my paranoia showed itself as a sudden rage, and I would become highly confrontational. She says, "It was like your whole mood just turned on a pin." I would accuse my parents of not caring for me and shout and scream at them. I would demand they drop everything they were doing and listen to whatever it was I was ranting about. I would say, "You never do anything for me! You never even try to help or understand me! You don't think that I know things, but I do. You never do anything to understand or help me!" I'd accuse them of being the worst parents in the world. One time, when my mum was visiting me in hospital, I lifted my head, stared coldly at her and said, "Why do you always lie to me?" On a couple of occasions, I have smashed things too – sorry, Mum and Far – which is *sooooooo* not who I am, nor how I normally behave. My mum says that paranoia is the one aspect of the illness that she finds the most challenging to deal with. She says that she has learned to "step away from it" when I am being paranoid, and she will calmly say to me, "Georgia, I love you and I know that this is your illness talking, but I will not speak to your paranoia. Either you need to leave the room, or I will – because I will not be spoken to like this, and I will not tolerate this behaviour. You know that nobody loves you more than your father and I, and we will always be here for you, but I will not negotiate with paranoia. So, you need to step away until you feel that you are ready to talk to me calmly, and then I will do everything I can to help you." My mum can handle anything.

When I was at my most ill, paranoia made me believe that what my voices said was fact, that people really were saying and thinking horrible things about me. After all, I'd heard voices all my life – and they'd started out nice – so why wouldn't I believe them when they were saying things that were horrible? Paranoia can be extremely debilitating if not kept in check, no matter how it manifests itself, and it can take its toll on the whole family if allowed to run rampant.

I hope this chapter provided you with a little insight into what it is.

CHAPTER 10
AMBIVALENCE

As fellow typeface nerds will know, choosing a font is a delicate process. I alternate between being able to use the same font for months on end or changing it at least 15 times before finally deciding on one – and then switching again! There is no in-between in this process.

It's the same with my blog design. I would *never* have got started if I hadn't forced myself to "Just. Pick. SOMETHING!" I finally chose a water theme, having reasoned that nothing was really a "perfect" backdrop for content about schizophrenia. On the other hand, maybe a picture of a brain – or a graphic representation of nasty voices – would set the tone I wanted? Or not? Maybe it would be too dark? Or not? Maybe water would be irrelevant? Or not?

All of this brings me to the subject of this chapter: ambivalence.

Ambivalence is a common symptom of schizophrenia. Ambivalence is not just conflicting feelings about a given choice, it is a pervasive, all-encompassing trait that has a major impact on the sufferer's life. It spans from coming to a standstill about which jam to choose in the supermarket to more important things, like whether to get out of bed, shower, visit a friend or pay a bill.

The number of times I've vacillated over minor decisions is more than I care to admit. Ambivalence is embarrassing – how do you explain you were late to an appointment because you couldn't decide which socks to wear? Really, truly could not force yourself to make a decision about a pair of socks! Even though logic tells you, "It doesn't matter what blooming socks you wear!" Even though you know you are going to be extremely late, you cannot get your brain to make that choice. You're blank. Frozen. Incapable. Sometimes, when I am standing at the shower, I cannot make the decision to turn the water on. I just stand there, zombie-like, unable to move, unable to make that choice. I feel pathetic and weak, like I won't ever succeed in life because I can't even succeed at making a simple decision. At least, that's how I feel about it – or I think it is. Wait a minute... *is* it? Do I feel that way about it? *Aaaaaaaaaaargh*! It is agony.

Now, I know it's not exactly a life-threatening condition, and perhaps "agony" is being a bit dramatic, but I do tend to get thrown into a dark place if I feel I've made a wrong decision. My mind can be set off by something as inconsequential as sending a birthday message to a friend or posting a photo to Instagram, especially if I can't take it back – commitment is scary! I need to remind myself that I am not doing anything wrong. In the big scheme of things, none of these actions really matter. What matters is how you treat others and make them feel – your morals and behaviour – not whether your birthday message is a bit random or your Instagram photo is not interesting enough.

Sometimes, I will be hit by a surge of overwhelming regret when I think about choices I've made in the past, even choices I was happy with at the time. This unease is difficult to deal with, particularly as paranoia tends to turn up at exactly these moments! How can I possibly move forward in my life when I still ruminate over a coat I donated to charity in 2008 and deeply regret giving away because it was a treasured gift from my dad (even though I had never worn it... and it was for a very good cause)? It is difficult to assuage the overwhelming feelings of loss I still have because I let it go and wish I hadn't. Just thinking about it makes me feel terrible. I know it was a good thing to donate it. I know I was never going to wear it. But I cannot balance that against the feeling that I made the wrong choice. Ambivalence is the gift that keeps on giving!

I'm extremely sensitive to feeling like things aren't going in the right direction and, once a feeling plants itself, it's very difficult to stop it growing. I guess it's just a process, and it will take time, but I usually manage to find a way to get around the discomfort of believing that I am making the wrong decisions all the time.

I've found that, over time, I can somehow find a way to justify my past choices to myself. *Of course* I sent that message – I meant it sincerely at the time. *Of course* I bought that pair of shoes – they're fabulous and I love wearing them. *Of course* I didn't go to that party – it would just have stressed me out. Naturally, we can never know the alternative outcome of our choices, but who's to say that the decision you make today might not lead to something better tomorrow?

One of my all-time favourite films, *Notting Hill*, gives us some food for thought. The main character William Thacker makes a decision that almost turns out to be the wrong one: he turns down Anna's request to resume their relationship. Fortunately, with his friends' help, he changes his decision, and the film concludes happily. So, yes, it is entirely possible to royally mess up and make wrong decisions – but it's also possible to amend them.

In general, you don't want to act rashly and regret it later, but neither should you overthink things and end up being paralysed by ambivalence.

Of course, as someone who overthinks things all the time – but somehow also manages to make a ton of spontaneous decisions where I later ask myself, "What was I *thinking*?" – I am hardly an expert in this area. I do hope, however, that my musings on this topic can help you gain clarity and insight into your own decision-making processes and, if you'd like to know what other strategies I use to deal with ambivalence, I have noted them later in this book ("Coping Strategies", page 143).

But, for now, onto my next chapter…

CHAPTER 11
CATATONIA

I have experienced catatonia three times. The first two happened on separate occasions (but in the exact same situation): aged seven, I was playing with one of my best friends. We had eaten dinner and were having a lovely time when, suddenly, out of nowhere, I couldn't move. The attack seemed to last forever but, with some effort, I managed to resist my body's lack of cooperation and force myself to stand up. My limbs felt like lead, and I couldn't say goodbye when her parents came to collect her. Strangely, I didn't mention it to my parents. I suppose, being so young, I dismissed it as something normal – how was I to know? – and, as I wasn't in great pain or distress, why mention it? I think I just thought, "Huh? Weird…" and, once the moment had passed, forgot about it.

I experienced catatonia later in life in connection with my breakdown. I would lie in bed for hours on end, staring into the wall, unable to move or speak. However, this was connected to hearing so many voices (200 of them) and being utterly engulfed by that noise. I clearly remember the two episodes I had in my childhood due to the intense feeling of heaviness in my whole body, my inability to speak and the horror I felt at being unable to un-stick myself. Why was this happening? What would I say to my friend if she noticed I was frozen like a block of ice? What could I say when I had apparently lost the power of speech? What would I do if it happened again while I was the goalkeeper in netball practice?

At that age, I likened my paralysis to being frozen by an Ice Pokémon attack (as I'd seen many times in my Game Boy games). It was frightening to me – so, perhaps relating it to Pokémon was my way of normalizing and coping with it.

CHAPTER 12
HOSPITAL

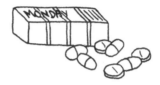

My time in hospital was a peaceful experience.

As mentioned in an earlier chapter, I spent the first three months in the 'closed' unit which, at the time, seemed mightily unfair and exasperatingly boring, but I know now it was necessary.

Back then, I was enraged that I'd been taken away from my normal life. I couldn't understand why I had to be in a psychiatric ward, especially as the only patient in the closed unit – separated from the other patients by a locked glass door – with nothing to do. What had I done to be treated this way?! Why did I have to take this antipsychotic medicine? I didn't have access to a computer so I couldn't even talk to my friends or classmates and tell them where I was. During the period of my breakdown, my friends had all expressed their concerns for me, which I couldn't understand at the time. Several of my classmates had messaged me to ask why I wasn't in school, but I hadn't replied. No matter how desperate I felt for social contact, I didn't have the mental energy to cope with it.

I often insisted on speaking to my psychiatrist just to feel I had some sort of control over my own day. I would say only two things: "I'm not supposed to be here!" and "When will you let me out?" Needless to say, he couldn't provide the answers I wanted to hear.

I had been sectioned and couldn't yet grasp the extent of my illness – lack of insight into one's illness is a common problem with psychosis.

According to what my psychiatrist told my parents, I was "an unusual case". He'd been a practising psychiatrist for many years and, in his experience, had seen less than ten cases like me. I will try to explain it as best as I remember: basically, he said that in most cases of schizophrenia, the individual is overwhelmed and swallowed up by the disease, but in my case, I was "still there". At my core, there was still a semblance of Georgia. However – and this is where it gets tricky – the Georgia that was there was one of my own creation: I had put her together myself during my childhood in order to be acceptable to my peers. My mum told me that, when I was very young, she noticed that I always observed other children and mirrored their behaviour in order to fit in. In this way, I had (unconsciously) built a Georgia that I thought was how I was supposed to be – and it was *that* Georgia struggling to fight her way through the psychosis. I hope that makes sense, and I hope that I have explained it correctly. I should reiterate at this point that this is *my* understanding of what the psychiatrist told me – he might have a much more medically intricate explanation.

Anyway, back to the hospital…

After the first two weeks, when the hospital told my parents that they should not visit me to afford me total rest, they came to visit me daily. Initially, I was very angry with them, but as the medicine began to work and the whole situation cooled off, my rage and indignation began to subside. After some time, we began to take short walks in the area surrounding the hospital. The hospital is located on the western side of the fjord, close to the harbour and charming fishermen's cottages. During my seven months in hospital, we spent many hours meandering through the little streets and through the hospital grounds. To vary our route, we would sometimes go through the grassy fields behind the hospital and walk directly down to the fjord.

The youth psychiatric ward at the hospital was called *Fjorden* (the Fjord). The building's design was bright and welcoming whilst also being a secure environment for people who were severely mentally ill.

Patients who were 18 and older were treated in a different building, and the criminally insane were housed in a totally separate, high-security area. My room in the closed unit was spacious and had its own bathroom, although I couldn't have told you that in the throes of my psychosis. I don't remember much about the décor apart from the curtains, which were blue and orange in a kind of diamond pattern. There was a living room with a TV and sofas next to the eating area. All cutlery was made of plastic and locked away when not in use – in fact, all cupboards and drawers had locks on them. If patients were brought flowers, they would be put in a rubber vase, not a glass one. These measures were put in place to protect the most vulnerable patients who might try to harm themselves or attack the staff.

The nurses were all very kind, and their care and support during my darkest time was fantastic. Really, they were wonderful. All of them. I couldn't have asked for a better level of care during my stay at Fjorden. They were attentive, gentle, helpful, endlessly patient and just went the extra mile to look after me in a time when I could barely string two words together, let alone think about my well-being.

Lovely as the nurses were, however, there was one area where I wouldn't cooperate with them: I would not take my medicine. I refused – point-blank – for two weeks! After much calm explanation on the part of the medical staff and my parents, I finally agreed to take it. However, I insisted on reading *all* the printed paperwork that came with it. You know those notes inside the box that nobody ever bothers with? I read every single word, including the long list of side effects! In the end, it was decided that I would take Risperdal because I couldn't swallow the massive Seroquel pills – why on earth do they make those pills so large? I remember that Risperdal, which I was given in a melting-tablet form, tasted of mint and started to have an effect on my psychosis within a few weeks.

My parents began seeing the first small glimpses of progress in my recovery after this time. However, I also experienced a wide range of side effects. First of all, I gained a lot of weight – my appetite increased significantly because the medicine removed my ability to feel full. I got restless leg syndrome, a very unpleasant sensation which constantly made me feel the need to get up and move around. My nose became stuffy, my mouth dry and, worst of all, I suffered from involuntary eye-rolling, a common and unpleasant side effect of antipsychotics. It sounds like something a sulky teenager would do, but it's a horrible experience. You are unable to control your eyes as they forcefully roll upward, forcing your head to tilt back in the process. Not only that, but this affected my tongue, too! It began to thrust forward and out of the mouth, making me feel like I was going to throw up. The name given to these side effects is an oculogyric crisis. Fortunately, my mum was visiting when it kicked off, so we quickly informed a nurse, and she gave me a dose of Akineton, a medicine designed to stop the effects of my oculogyric crisis. I still take Akineton today when needed. It takes effect after 10–20 minutes, which sounds fast on paper but feels like a lifetime when you're in the middle of an eye-rolling attack on public transport! I'm not complaining, though – I'm just glad Akineton exists.

Today, I seem to have found the correct balance of medicine for me: I take Abilify and Zyprexa. My doctors would prefer that I was not on two antipsychotic medications at the same time, but when my Abilify dose was increased, I experienced much worse eye-rolling, and when my Zyprexa dose was increased, I gained a substantial amount of weight again. As I didn't feel happy being a heavy eye-roller, it was decided that a combination of Abilify and Zyprexa would work best for me.

While I was in the closed unit, I was prescribed sertraline for a while, a generic antidepressant meant to enhance the effect of my antipsychotic medicine. In my case, it didn't have the predicted effect, so it was withdrawn from my medication plan.

As a patient, it's important to find the balance of medicine that *you* can live with: a dose that relieves your symptoms but gives you as few side effects as possible.

Eventually, after three months, I was allowed into the open unit, where I could meet the other patients. It was a gradual process, and I still had my room in the closed unit to use when I needed alone time. Meeting the other patients – there were about seven or eight of us in total – was overwhelming, but they were also young people like me, facing problems of their own. Some had schizophrenia, others had depression, eating disorders, borderline personality disorder. We were all just teenagers struggling to come to terms with our diagnoses.

The ward had a school, although I didn't attend it until much later in my hospital stay. It consisted of two teachers. We would be given Danish and maths assignments, work on an art project or watch films. I enjoy solving arithmetic problems – so much so that one of the other patients said to me, "Wow, there's definitely nothing wrong with *that* area of your brain!" I loved this comment – even though I was unable to show it at the time – because it was positive and funny and went a little way to reassuring me that at least some of my brain was still functioning correctly. I may have been incapable of speaking and connecting with others, but at least my intellect and drive to use it were both still vaguely intact!

When I was eventually transferred to the open unit, things were slightly different: I now ate breakfast and participated in morning meetings with the other patients. After the morning meeting, we'd go to school, followed by lunch. After that, the rest of our day was free until dinner time, apart from some snack breaks in between. The food at the hospital was good and freshly made every day by the ward's cook. In the evening we had a communal meeting to talk about how our day had been, and then we had free time again until bedtime at 10pm.

In the open unit, there was a whiteboard in the nurses' office that had each patient's primary doctor and nurse written on it. I noticed that I was the only one with the chief psychiatrist as my primary doctor, which made me feel a bit special – the star pupil! Of course, I was no such thing, but, as my parents always joke with me, "If you're going to do mental illness, you might as well do it really well!"

I wasn't diagnosed with paranoid schizophrenia immediately. In fact, I was first diagnosed as schizotypal. It was only shortly before I was discharged from hospital that I received my final diagnosis. This is because a psychiatrist needs to observe his or her patient over a substantial period to make an accurate diagnosis. They also need to rule out the possibility that the patient's issues might be in connection to physical conditions in the brain, such as a tumour. During the first weeks of my hospital stay, I was taken for an MRI scan to rule out the possibility of a brain tumour. Thankfully, the scan was clear – and I "only" have schizophrenia!

Funnily enough, my eventual diagnosis came as a relief to me. Finally, I had an explanation for why I'd struggled socially *all* my life. I had never been able to understand why my peers were so capable of forming relationships when I wasn't. What made me so different? Why did I struggle with forward-planning, memory and the most basic tasks? Aha, so *that* was why. Yes, the diagnosis made a lot of things fall into place for me, not least the voices that I'd been hearing since childhood.

I was to stay in the hospital for seven months. During that time, I was allowed home visits in small doses: first on Wednesdays, then on Wednesdays and weekends. The reason for this staggered approach is to ensure that you can cope with the change in your routine. As I've mentioned before, any form of stress is potentially harmful, even the positive stress of going home and spending time with the family.

Just prior to leaving hospital, my younger brother Oliver came to visit me. My parents had sheltered Ollie from a lot of what was "going on with Georgia" but, once things started to improve, they believed it would be healthy and useful for him to see for himself where I was staying so that he might have a better understanding and not be worried about it. In fact, Mum told me that it was Oliver who asked her if he could come and visit me, and she agreed that would be a good idea.

When I was hospitalized, I didn't have any pre-conceived ideas about what to expect – frankly, I wasn't well enough to think about it – so it was interesting (and funny) to hear Ollie's take on his first-time visit to a psychiatric hospital. Ollie told us he'd expected something completely different to what he saw at the ward. In his mind, he'd envisaged something like *One Flew Over the Cuckoo's Nest,* the 1970s film starring Jack Nicholson – and maybe also an element of *The Shining*'s "Here's Johnny!" He also thought that the hospital would be a spartan, sterile and foreboding "prison" echoing with the sounds of wailing patients as they shuffled mindlessly in straitjackets and chains. He was greatly relieved to discover that the reality was a calm and welcoming environment with sympathetic nurses, warmth and hugs, and shackle-free patients… he even saw a friend of his. Although we still laugh about Ollie's pre-visit imaginings, it does serve to illustrate the misconceptions even the kindest and most well-intentioned of people still have about psychiatric hospitals and the patients within them.

REALITY CHECK

WHAT YOU SEE:

A young woman going out of her way to avoid charity fundraisers trying to approach her on the street.

WHAT'S ACTUALLY HAPPENING:

I'm in town to collect my medicine, nothing else. Just a short trip to the pharmacy and back home. It takes so much of my energy to go into town that I can't face doing anything else – not even the colourful clothes hanging outside my favourite shop can tempt me. There are so many tiny, trivial interactions involved in a short trip like this that I can't have anything interrupting the end goal.

Just entering the pharmacy is a nerve-wracking moment. Pressing the screen for a queueing number and trying to look relaxed and normal as I wait takes much thought and self-control. When I say, "Hi, I would like to collect my Abilify," to the pharmacist – did I say it right? – it is boundary-breaking and stressful. Inserting my payment card into the machine while avoiding eye contact and not speaking might appear rude, but I need to focus on paying the pharmacist, not dropping my card from shaking hands, panicking that someone will see my PIN and remembering to say "thank you" at the end – manners maketh the man! Have I done it all right? Do I look like a normal person? Have I said anything weird or wrong or stupid? Are people staring at me and thinking, "Who's that weirdo?" Finally, it's over, and I can smile with relief as I gather my things up again, ensuring that I have taken my card and receipt, have everything I need and have said "thank you" (again!) to the pharmacist before exiting the pharmacy, whereupon I will check my bag *again* once I'm outside, just to reassure myself that I have done everything correctly.

This was the reality for many years – I almost never left the house because it all seemed so insurmountable, and suddenly being approached by a charity spokesperson would just add to my list of stresses.

CHAPTER 13
STRESS

So, what's the deal with stress?

For a long time, I wondered why I'd had a relapse on 1 January 2015 because I'd been doing great up to that point. My everyday life with part-time work and ceramics had been going well, and I was managing some social stuff with my friends. I'd jumped into the new year surrounded by people I love when – BOOM! – the next day, I slid into the depths of the abyss.

Again.

As if it wasn't enough to be psychotic once.

Talk about starting the new year with a bang!

It was then that it struck me: I had been aware of an increase in voices for a while, the negative kind. Aha! I should have paid more attention to that but, to be honest, everyone said I was doing fantastically, *I* felt I was doing fantastically, and I had even been discharged from OPUS, a treatment option in Denmark for anyone who experiences symptoms of a psychosis for the first time. I started in OPUS immediately after I was discharged from the psychiatric ward. You are assigned a psychiatric nurse whom you visit regularly. There are various courses that you can take, such as social skills training, education in the disease and family group, all of which take place with other young people who have had a psychosis. I participated in most of them. On being discharged from OPUS, I was then referred to a local psychiatrist instead of being under the umbrella care of District Psychiatry.

This was a really good sign, because it showed that I was now being considered as less dependent on the system. So, I'd relaxed a bit and was taking for granted that my progress would continue, without keeping a more attentive eye on any symptoms. Oops. Unfortunately, the voices come sneaking up on you when you least expect it. This may sound strange, but I'm not always so aware of them at the time I get them. It is often later – for example, when my mum asks, "Have you had any voices lately?" – that I might register they've been there. It is frustrating that I don't always notice them, but also a relief that I can switch off from them every now and then. I guess I can't be on alert for voices 24/7 (it's incredibly stressful), but the result is that those pesky voices sometimes sneak in without me realizing they have become more persistent. Fortunately, I'm now much more aware of the level of my voices and use them as a sort of stress-alert alarm to warn me to slow down and take care of myself.

I would like to share with you some of the things from my OPUS course that I found helpful:

Stress-Vulnerability Model

Yup, here it is again...

The Stress-Vulnerability Model, which was originally developed by two American psychiatrists, Joseph Zubin and Bonnie Spring, shows the relationship between stress and the development of psychosis. We all know about negative stress from conflicts, quarrels, strict deadlines, etc. But positive stress also exists. It may not weigh as much on the illness scales as negative stress does, but one must be careful anyway. Positive stress (also known as eustress) can arise from socializing with friends, excitement or anticipation, or major life events, such as romantic relationships. It can also be triggered simply by being exposed to lots of stimuli: for example, going to a concert or festival, or going for a walk around town.

For me, positive stress manifests itself as positive or neutral voices.

I think this kind of stress is inevitable in daily life and, unless you're isolated at home and never make contact with the outside world, you will experience positive stress. So, what can one do to try to reduce its negative effects?

STRESS FACTORS / PROTECTIVE FACTORS

Where some stress factors might include traumatic events, conflicts, sleep deprivation, social isolation or drug misuse, examples of protective factors include taking your prescribed medicine, having constructive sessions with your psychiatric nurse and surrounding yourself with a strong, supportive network. It is important to outweigh damaging stress factors with protective factors. There are many more protective factors than mentioned in the above list – it is really just about finding the things that make you happy, relaxed and comfortable in your own skin. Exercise releases endorphins and reduces anxiety, so you should try your best to put it on the list, even if you can only manage a short walk every other day. Listening to music is also a good bet. Sometimes it helps to listen to sad music when you're sad and angry music when you're angry. For me, it helps to validate those feelings. At other times it might be better to listen to slightly more upbeat music to achieve peace of mind – or even classical music, which is proven to reduce stress.

Personally, my protective factors are:

- Writing (surprise, surprise!)
- Listening to my favourite music

- Seeing my friends – but not too much
- Sleeping (I think that counts as a protective factor for everybody, healthy people included)
- Drawing
- Painting
- Ceramics
- Relaxing in front of my computer

But how does this information correspond with the previous point? Didn't I just say that too much positive stress is bad, too? Why yes, I did – and that still holds true. The nature of schizophrenia is such that you are sometimes forced to live a more restricted life than other people. I can't cope with too much negativity and tension, just as I can't cope with too much excitement and input. So, as I will discuss in a later chapter, something like being in a relationship is probably out of the question for me at the moment, as is trying to reach some of my bigger personal ambitions. It can be disheartening, but I'm coming to terms with it because my health and stress threshold are the most important factors in my recovery. I realize that, for now, I need to sacrifice some of the other aspects of my life to ensure I stay as healthy as I possibly can. It's tough, but for me, that's just the way it has to be. Every day I work toward becoming more robust. It's my top priority. This doesn't make me less dedicated or determined to succeed – just human. We are naturally drawn to what makes us happy or provides us with comfort. However, when you have schizophrenia, you must be cautious about getting too much of a good thing. I've learned that I have to seek out only what won't disrupt my fragile mind. On the other hand, something like writing doesn't trigger these disruptive happy hormones in the way that socializing and goal-setting do – or, at least, not for me. My favourite thing to do is write: it's solitary, therapeutic, clears my mind and is relaxing rather than over-stimulating. With writing, I don't have to overthink. It comes naturally. I love it. It has saved my life.

With this chapter, my aim is to illustrate how to protect yourself from different types of stress in a way that I hope will provide recognition and understanding for others in the same situation. It would make me so happy if my words reached and helped those who need it. I know I would have benefited greatly from something similar in the early years of my diagnosis and recovery.

IMPORTANT ADVICE: I must state that it's very important to listen to yourself and the potential returning of symptoms. Always tell trusted loved ones if you feel you're slipping back into illness. Don't assume that, just because you haven't *felt* stressed, you're okay. That was my mistake. I was looking in the wrong places for signs and unwittingly ignoring the real red flags – my voices. I'm not saying that you should completely freak yourself out and think you're going to relapse tomorrow, but just be aware that stress, both good and bad, can have repercussions on your mental health. As mentioned, I felt great prior to my relapse, but I am fairly convinced that it was positive stress that caused it to happen. As a result, I have learned to use my chosen protective factors as a means of controlling how life impacts me and my fragile brain.

CHAPTER 14
AVOLITION

Motivation is a funny thing, isn't it?

In schizophrenia, there are three main groups of symptoms: positive, negative and cognitive. Positive, in this context, means symptoms that *arise* due to the illness (i.e. they're not present in healthy individuals), while negative refers to behaviours that are taken away by the illness.

Positive symptoms include visual or auditory hallucinations and delusions, such as paranoid thinking.

Negative symptoms include the flat effect, or reduced facial emotion; alogia, also known as poverty of speech; anhedonia, which means loss of pleasure; and avolition, a lack of motivation.

Avolition is different from procrastination. It might be described like this: it's like you really want to get something done, but you are incapable of summoning up the mental and physical motivation to do it. Even though you fully understand that the repercussions of your inaction will create consequences that you dread or don't want to deal with, you are completely unable to do what you want to do.

Avolition has been, and continues to be, a major source of frustration for me. Being a naturally driven and ambitious person and having to deal with the limitations my illness imposes on me is a devastating combination. I have dreams and goals just like the next person, but I sometimes lack the competencies to see them through to completion.

It's not just the big goals, like what I want to do with my life. Avolition also impairs my ability to carry out smaller everyday tasks and interactions that, no matter which way you look at them, have a deadline. Getting out of bed in the morning? Preparing and eating something for breakfast? Showering? Choosing an outfit and getting dressed? I haven't even gone out the door yet, and there are already so many things in which I've had to invest my limited energy!

I'm not saying I struggle with these things all the time, but when my personal resources are low, it's a different story. When I'm feeling stronger, I don't have so much of a problem with avolition. However, I still struggle with replying to messages and emails, often taking days, if not weeks, to get back to people. It once took me three months to book an appointment with a skin clinic – which required one phone call – and that was fast for me! I can never *just* reply or *just* decide or *just* get it done – there's always a process involved. I'm happier deferring a decision than finalizing it. Unfortunately, it's not just me who's affected by this; the people around me can get driven up the wall by my perceived slowness! With schizophrenia, there's no sense of urgency, which could explain why I'm often late, despite my best efforts not to be. The thing is, I do eventually get around to it – just at my own avolition-influenced pace.

All this, of course, is very demotivating. Can I really call myself a professional artist if I can't complete my commissions more efficiently? Will I ever become a mature adult when I struggle with many of the basics of real life? Will my friends eventually tire of my fear-based reluctance to take the train to Copenhagen to visit them? (So many impressions and things to think about: check in, check out, avoiding eye contact with other passengers, where to sit, crowds, noise, etc.) There are so many aspects of life that are affected by schizophrenia, and avolition is one of the culprits. So, we can just add that to voices, paranoia, high sensitivity to stress, ambivalence and communication difficulties.

Avolition regret

One thing that often bothers me is the fact that I had to turn down the most unique offer I've ever had: an offer to be an apprentice to a well-known Danish porcelain artist. Maria is a family friend and, having read my Danish blog, wrote to me to say she'd love it if I could come to her studio – entirely on my own terms – and help her with her work. I could work on my own, or whatever I wanted to do. Completely chill – no pressure whatsoever. Maria is internationally successful and brilliant at what she does, and her offer was something I knew she didn't give to just anyone. I knew it was special. I knew it was a one-of-a-kind opportunity.

I just couldn't do it.

I went to her studio in Copenhagen a few times, but I found it too difficult to cope with. The journey to Copenhagen was tiring and stressful since I cannot drive and need to use public transport. Walking along the long, busy road toward her studio was overwhelming due to the noise, people and so many different impressions to take in. On arrival at her studio, I was supposed to let her know I'd arrived – but I would wait silently downstairs until she came down, paralysed on the spot. As for making conversation, unfortunately, I would only answer questions when asked and was never able to initiate a conversation.

A simple task like pressing clay into moulds proved too demanding because I got confused and couldn't remember what my assignments were, despite them being clearly and patiently explained to me every time. I was incredibly slow and anxious, not confident in my approach at all. Sadly, despite Maria's kindness and patience, I had to make the decision to stop. I am still so sad about it, because I know what an incredible opportunity wonderful Maria had given me. Maybe in the future, I'll be robust enough to cope with opportunities like that, but life doesn't always work out the way I want… *sigh*. Thanks a lot, avolition. #HeavySarcasm

Maybe everyone feels this way, schizophrenia or not. Perhaps it's part of the human condition to feel like we're never living up to our full potential. We all have our struggles and obstacles, whether they're physical, mental or circumstantial.

Seen from a broader perspective, I'm doing okay, but recovery is not linear. Sometimes it's two steps forward, one step back. Sometimes you realize the path you thought you were destined to take wasn't for you after all, so you need to take the slower, scenic route. Recovery shouldn't be so complicated that you feel overwhelmed, but you need to be prepared for the fact that it will have its challenges.

In any case, my avolition is a grain of sand on the beach of existence. It's not a joy to live with, but it's not the end of the world, either. As long as I'm fundamentally content with life and not in chronic pain or distress, I won't complain about falling short on occasion. There are many wonderful things about life – and, hopefully, I'll grow old and have the privilege of experiencing them all.

CHAPTER 15
COMMUNICATION

The greatest frustration I've had throughout my life is difficulties with communication.

I can write blog posts about my own experiences with relative ease but, when it comes to text messages and emails, I am completely blank. I don't know what questions to ask or how to craft an articulate message. As for verbal and social communication, they're a total nightmare. There are two reasons why I avoid making small talk at the supermarket check-out: either the words simply won't materialize in my head, or something happens on the way out and they become a mumbled, bumbled, jumbled mess – and that makes me wonder how I've ever managed to make any friends!

The wonderful friends who I did manage to make accept all this about me. They always try to find the positive and say things like, "Maybe you find communication difficult, but look at the drawings you can create! I wish I could do that." They see me for who I am and encourage me to feel more confident in my own abilities. They are a truly special group of girls and have stuck with me through everything – good, bad and psychotic. I cannot over-stress how important their friendship and loyalty are to me. They are the best.

Communication when you have schizophrenia is challenging. If the weekly sessions I had in social skills training are anything to go by, the struggle to regain the conversational skills that psychosis has smashed to pieces is a common one.

I remember being told of a film where the main character learns how to talk by echoing other people's speech. He can only repeat the words he hears them say. Unfortunately, I can't remember what the film was called, but I can imagine how confusing it would be for his contemporaries.

"Would you like an apple?"

"Apple!" *Vigorous pointing*

Okaaaaaaaaay, then…

That's how I would describe what it can be like to communicate when you have schizophrenia. After my first psychotic episode, I had to re-learn everything from scratch – communication skills, practical skills, basic life skills, everything.

As mentioned, one way to learn is to observe and, after my breakdown, I needed to get back into a social environment where I could watch others' behaviour and try to absorb natural ways of communicating. There were so many people that I wanted to get to know better, and I felt I was rubbish at connecting with them. Today, I'm far more relaxed about communication and, paradoxically, it has become easier. There wasn't a sudden, earth-shattering insight that magically cured all my social awkwardness, just a moment of realization when I thought, "Hey, I *can* do this. Why did I ever think I couldn't?" However, this newsflash came after years of being included at all family events even though I was mostly silent, having constant communication with my parents and brother and extended family, reconnecting with my closest friends, and exposing myself to the outside world and all the communication that entails. It took observation and practice, practice, practice! I had to force myself to do it. However, my family and friends provided enormous back-up by always talking with me no matter how disjointed and unfocused the conversations might have been, and by finding ways that I could try to improve my social skills whilst always being there to protect me, guide me or lead me gently back to the path of coherent communication.

It's important to expose oneself to social situations even if you don't think it will ever help. It will. The more you participate in social situations – as long as you don't push yourself too far – the more insight and savvy you'll gain. This may come much easier to you than it did to me, depending on whether you're normally a gregarious extrovert or a happy recluse who just happens to have great social skills! However, it's also vital that you listen to yourself, and if you're not motivated to practise your communication skills, don't do it. There's no right or wrong way to be – we all have different needs when it comes to our social lives, self-expression and feelings of achievement. I recommend asking a family member or trusted friend to stick with you at social events and using them as your safety net if you need help with conversation.

I know I can communicate perfectly fine when in an environment where I feel safe. Right now, I'm working on being able to talk more freely in situations where I don't necessarily feel 100 per cent comfortable all the time (e.g. making small talk with a cashier). Otherwise, I fear I would never speak outside of my family and friend groups. I'm trying to be more consistent in communicating – saying "good morning" to my ceramics group, then following up with a "how are you?" – listening, nodding, being engaged in the conversation and building up from there. I'm more able to say something with humour and ask relevant questions than before, and I sense people respond well to it, so much better than they did to the total silence of the early years after my breakdown.

What I'm trying to say is, although it may take *years*, as it has for me, I think it's entirely possible to feel more confident and capable when it comes to communication. I think we all have it in us, it just needs to be unlocked.

CHAPTER 16
ANTIPSYCHOTICS AND SIDE EFFECTS

Antipsychotic medication is a vital component of recovery. It reduces and relieves symptoms allowing your brain to breathe, reset and restore itself, and you can then focus on getting better without background noise hindering your progress. This requires patience – it can take up to six weeks before you start to feel any difference – and a few months before you feel the full effect of the medicine.

It's important that you do not stop taking the medication as soon as you start to feel better. Let me just repeat that: it's important that you do not stop taking the medication as soon as you start to feel better! Antipsychotics work in the long term, so coming off them abruptly increases your risk of relapse. As a result, you may have to take a higher dose, and this can result in more severe side effects, which I will elaborate on shortly.

For some people, finding an antipsychotic that works for them – as prescribed by their psychiatrist – is a relatively quick and unproblematic process. Others may need to try several different drugs, or combinations of medicines, before they find the right one.

Okay, now for the (slightly) scary bit…

Common side effects of antipsychotics include dizziness, sedation, weight gain, restless legs, dry mouth, stuffy nose, lactation (production of breast milk), heart palpitations, muscle spasms, eye-rolling, blurred vision, body temperature regulation problems and increased sensitivity to sunlight. There is also a risk of developing neuroleptic malignant syndrome, a rare but serious disorder that affects your nervous system; and tardive dyskinesia, jerky or twisting movements of the face or body. Again, these conditions are rare, but important to keep an eye out for.

And… *breathe…*

Many medicines can have side effects, so weighing up the benefits and drawbacks of your treatment is essential. Can you live with the side effects if your schizophrenia symptoms are kept at bay? Or are your side effects causing additional distress? Speak to your psychiatrist or healthcare provider – they can probably prescribe a medicine for your side effects, or help you find a different antipsychotic that suits you better.

It is very important to work with your healthcare providers until you find a solution that works well for you.

QUICK QUESTION:

How do you feel about people always confusing schizophrenia with multiple personality disorder?

A bit frustrated, but no more than that.

To be honest, I had no clue what schizophrenia was before I fell ill, so I don't expect everyone to know the ins and outs of it. However, it would be nice if people were a little more informed these days since mental illness awareness is so publicly advocated. So, just to be clear, SCHIZOPHRENIA HAS NOTHING TO DO WITH MULTIPLE PERSONALITIES! Multiple personality disorder is a completely different diagnosis.

Okay? Got it? Good.

CHAPTER 17
THE PENCIL

It's time to talk about bullying.

I've already described a little bit about what bullies did to me, but now I'll go in depth about my experiences with this toxic behaviour and its effects on the victim.

Bullying is generally defined as recurrent acts of cruel behaviour by an individual or group, targeting a less powerful individual or group with the intent to cause harm – physical, emotional or psychological. Physical bullying involves actual physical attacks: hitting, punching and kicking, for example. Emotional bullying involves using words to hurt the victim. Psychological bullying is the use of control tactics to mess with the victim's mind. All three types can overlap and exist simultaneously.

In my teenage years, I didn't talk to anyone about the bullying I experienced. I was young, already desperately lonely, and I didn't want to draw attention to my perceived social inadequacy. I listened to music and wrote poems instead.

Being bullied is a real psychological burden with consequences that cannot be overstated. The victim can develop a whole host of psychological issues – depression, anxiety, self-harm, suicidal thoughts and worse – or experience physical ailments, such as headaches, stomach problems or difficulty falling asleep. Finally, being bullied causes you to be deeply unhappy and unwilling to go to school or wherever the bullying takes place. Can you imagine how dreadful it feels for a young person, subject to compulsory education, to be *forced* to face their tormentor every single day? To have to deal with the torture and never being able to escape? Can you imagine the impact that has on a vulnerable young person? It eats away at your confidence, your psyche, until you eventually crack. What cracking looks like is different from person to person, but it's never pretty. The impact bullying has on an individual is increased when they don't have in-built resources to deal with it – such as the ability to think on the spot or use humour to deflect the bully – and *nobody* has the resources to deal with years of torment.

Bullying doesn't need to be obvious. Some of the most effective forms of bullying involve non-verbal tactics, like not acknowledging the victim's existence, also known as the silent treatment, a behaviour commonly experienced in female bullying. Being completely ostracized by one's peers is one of the most soul-destroying things that can happen to a human being because, if not to be included, heard and seen, what is the point of existing? I don't mean that in a morbid way; I just want to get the point across that everyone needs to feel that they are seen, otherwise they will start to wither away.

One of the many things my bullies did was completely ignore me when I tried to initiate contact. During school breaks, I would walk over to a group of my schoolmates – approaching them, for me, was a massive hurdle to overcome on its own – and *not one of them* would acknowledge my presence when I sat down. They would deliberately avoid eye contact and completely ignore me. Nobody said, "Hi, Georgia", smiled or made any attempt at friendliness. So, I would sit there awkwardly for ten minutes, eating my lunch as normally as I could manage, while they talked among themselves. If I summoned up the courage to make conversation, none of them would reply. They just went completely quiet – cue tumbleweed – and, after a very awkward pause, would continue their conversation as if I hadn't said anything at all.

As you can imagine, this was exceedingly difficult for me to deal with. I began to lose the will to keep trying. I even stopped making the effort to look nice every morning – what was the point? Nobody noticed when I'd come to school in a new denim jacket I really liked; in fact, my only memory of that particular day is one of the boys whispering to another, "She looks like a gorilla," while looking straight at me.

The final straw for me was when I was handed the remains of my favourite pencil – a lovely one my parents had brought back from Spain, and one that I knew I couldn't replace – and the bully said with a smirk, "Oops, I... accidentally broke it."

It had been snapped in half.

At the time, I was so desperate not to attract negative attention that I didn't get upset or angry. I knew it was intentional but didn't know how to deal with it. I felt that I'd be laughed at by my classmates if I made a fuss over a stupid pencil because they couldn't care less about my personal belongings, nor understand the sentiment attached. In any case, I kept my feelings to myself and slowly began to die inside. To this day, it hurts me to think about it.

In Year 9, there was a camping trip that couldn't have gone worse. Our accommodation consisted of four tents: two for the girls, two for the boys. One of the girls' tents could sleep eight, the other could sleep five, and I ended up in the smaller one. Unfortunately for me, nobody in this tent was making any attempt to be friendly or social. One of the girls (for whom "boyfriend troubles" was a permanent state) was crying, and her friend's method of comforting her was to shout at anyone who entered the tent. (*WTF?*) The third girl had retired to bed with a headache, and I felt so sorry for the fourth girl because she had only recently joined our class and must have thought that we were all a bunch of jerks. However, I was so caught up with my own worries that I just kept my mouth shut and tried to get through it all.

As stress from the shouting girl, drama from the crying girl and emotional tension from all the above had taken up residence in my tent, I decided to visit the other girls – a really huge step for me – in the hope of some relief. Once again, *none* of them spoke a word to me – totally ignored me. I felt completely out of my depth, unable to cope with their hostility and feeling like *I'd* done something wrong. As the chill of rejection filled the tent, one of the girls turned to me and cruelly said, "So, are you heading back to your own tent any time soon?"

Wow, that stung.

"Oh, okay," I said... and left.

Later that evening, I lay in the dark and thought, "Whose brilliant idea was it to do this camping trip?" I spent that night swamped by sadness, rage and confusion... unable to understand why my classmates would be so cruel.

(Note: the fourth girl in my tent left our class shortly afterwards. I completely understand why.)

During that period, I drove myself crazy trying to figure out what I was doing to provoke such horrible behaviour. Why were my classmates alternating between ignoring or tormenting me? Was I really such an awful person to be around?

With the wisdom of hindsight, I can see how cruelly they behaved, but when I was in it, I couldn't. However, I knew what it *felt* like. It is still painful to recall. Writing everything down has been a therapeutic exercise because it has helped me to understand that it wasn't my fault. I was the unwitting target of their nastiness. I didn't have the tools to fight back – and they knew it. I also know, to my cost, the many ways in which I've been held back by their toxic behaviour. Unfortunately, bullying creates a lifetime legacy of self-doubt.

To this day, none of them have apologized, nor were they ever reprimanded for their behaviour. The school claimed to have a "no bullying" policy, but, in my experience, the teachers just didn't want to know. They turned a blind eye to it all and, in doing so, allowed a child to suffer. The idea of addressing the issue never crossed their minds. In Danish schools, these anti-bullying stances are a joke. They do nothing about it. The lack of care was evident when my brother was picked on at the same school. This time, my parents were aware of it and approached the school on more than one occasion, and they were deeply unimpressed by the administration's indifference and lack of action. They were assured that the bullies' parents would be contacted and spoken to. This was patently untrue. As the bullying continued, my mother eventually contacted the relevant parents herself and was told that they had heard *nothing* from the school about their sons' behaviour. Not. A. Word.

It is a sobering thought that, even though society preaches that it has no tolerance for bullying, the responsible adults in charge of my class didn't do *anything* to stop it. Couldn't they see it? Couldn't they figure out that something was wrong? That the dynamics of the class were toxic? That I was hurting? Did they not learn this kind of thing during their training? I have many questions that could be applied to *any* given class in any school anywhere else in the world. What are schools actually DOING about bullying?

Workplace bullying exists too. It is a problem that should be addressed at its inception, before the bullying kids turn into bullying adults who are emboldened by the fact that they've never had any repercussion for their actions.

After Year 9, I decided to go to *efterskole*, which is a one-year boarding school you can choose to attend between Danish primary school and high school, usually with focus on creative and/or practical subjects, sports and the outdoors, alongside the normal school curriculum. I signed up for one about an hour's drive north of our home and looked forward to having a good year and meeting new people.

Little did I know that it would prove to be far worse than anything I had experienced up to that point.

On the first day, when our parents were present to help us get settled in, an extremely agitated girl was causing a commotion in the middle of the main hall. She was loud and angry, and the disruption did not go unnoticed, although everyone tried to politely ignore the overgrown toddler having a tantrum in the corner. We had been informed that school policy dictated that all rooms were shared and that we would each be allocated a dorm-mate. I remember thinking, "Oh my goodness, I hope *she's* not my roomie."

I think you know where this is going.

My parents and I headed to my allocated room and, on approaching it, could hear shouting and arguing. Guess who? The door was slightly ajar, and we realized that her father was the target of her rage. At that point, all I wanted to do was to back away and not face the tension on the other side of the door, but we had to go in and try to make the best of it. I said "hi" with as friendly a smile as I could manage, given that I was feeling out of my depth, and was met with a cold, silent stare from the girl. Her father told her to "say hello", at which point she said a sarcastic "hell-oooo", without the faintest trace of a smile or enthusiasm. I knew that I was screwed. Again.

I really tried my best to accommodate her volatile personality, but my efforts proved pointless. A few days in, after smoking outside with some guys from the school, she invited them to enter our room via the window directly above *my* bed. They did, leaving filthy, muddy footprints all over my pillow and duvet. She said nothing – in fact, she laughed and positively encouraged them. Very late at night, she would make a point of coming in and out of our room multiple times, slamming the door and encouraging her friends to talk loudly outside, sometimes banging on the door and shouting my name. One evening, it all got too much for me and I got up and locked the door – stupid, I know, but I just didn't know how else to cope.

All hell broke loose.

She started screaming that I was a "foul bitch" (and a lot worse) and began violently kicking the door until I could see it vibrate and splinter. I was upset, frightened and unsure what to do next, but I knew that opening the door again wasn't an option – her rage, as always, was completely out of proportion to the deed. I sat and waited until someone called a teacher, and only when I was sure that the girl wasn't there did I unlock the door.

After that, she was moved to a room with someone else.
And then someone else.

And then someone else.

Constantly repeating the same cycle of rage, drama and conflict.

In retrospect, I discovered that she was extremely unpopular. I think that most people were frightened of her uncontrolled rage and potty mouth, so they just played along for a peaceful life.

This wasn't the only incident of bullying that I endured. A few days into my stay, I started getting picked on by another girl who would loudly insult my taste in music and make fun of me in front of the other kids. On one occasion, she walked uninvited into my room and straight past me, then switched my music off. She would target me at every opportunity.

There was a small snack kiosk in the basement where one could buy sweets, crisps and other snacks. Whenever I was in the queue, this girl would roughly push in front of me in an apparent attempt to get a rise out of me. Every. Single. Time. I didn't have the confidence to say, "Hey, stop it!" and, apparently, neither did anyone else. Plus, I had the bonus of my ex-roomie from hell shooting me evil glares and announcing in a loud voice how she was going to "beat me up".

As the months passed, more and more pupils started tormenting and excluding me. A group of girls that I tried to hang out with always left the room the moment I entered it. Either they would stare at me in total silence until I felt compelled to leave, or they would all get up and go, only to return five minutes later once they had established that I had gone. Completely at a loss, I would return to my room, only to find that someone had covered the door handle with something slippery and spread sticky stuff on the floor. I was prevented from sleeping at night by people banging loudly on my bedroom window and running away. It was soul-destroying.

The final straw was an incident that happened when I was feeling unwell. I had been resting in my room all morning when, suddenly, the door was thrown open and a group of girls piled in – a couple of them holding cameras. Before I could do anything, they opened my wardrobe and threw my clothes about, rummaged in my drawers, flipped open my notebooks and diaries (and photographed what

I'd written inside them), took pictures of me, knocked things off my shelves and departed as quickly as they'd arrived.

I sat there bewildered. I had no idea what to do. Why had they taken the photos? What were they going to use them for? How could I go to them and say, "Please would you delete the photos?" They would have mocked me and laughed at me, and I didn't want to give them any more ammunition. How had they all collectively decided to do this to me? You can imagine how much all of that screwed with my mind. I felt completely powerless.

For a long time, I blamed myself: "I should never have chosen to go to that school. I shouldn't have brought notebooks. I shouldn't have tried to befriend those girls. I shouldn't have been so stupid."

I think it says something about this school that the exodus from it was substantial. My parents later discovered that it had a terrible reputation – it still does. Nearly all the nicer kids left the school early, citing their unhappiness. I managed to struggle on for a few months but, ultimately, the bullying from the poisonous posse took its toll, resulting in an emotional breakdown. My parents chose to remove me themselves.

Maybe one day I'll be free of the emotional impact of being bullied. I am still waiting.

CHAPTER 18
FAMILY

How can the family of a sufferer help their loved one?

I would say by learning about the illness, being available to talk, having endless patience and encouraging openness about one's diagnosis. As previously stated, I would never have come this far in my recovery without the extraordinary support and care from my family.

When I was in hospital, my parents visited daily – sometimes twice a day – and my mum read every book and online resource about schizophrenia she could find to try to understand what I was going through. My mum is a stay-at-home parent, and that proved to be a huge advantage in my recovery. For many years following my diagnosis, I needed 24/7 care and support because I was unable to leave the house on my own initiative. My mum is an extroverted introvert, if that makes sense. She appears outgoing and social but, in reality, she requires long periods alone to recoup and recharge, so it must have been a challenge for her to have me at home all the time! Not only was she there as my mother, but she also had to take on the role of on-call psychologist whenever I needed to have a deep talk, which was often and at any time of the day or night. In fact, not only did I regularly need to discuss my way through inner crises, but I also needed her help to send texts, emails and even Facebook updates because I simply couldn't muster the confidence to do it myself. I'm not just talking occasionally, I mean every single text, email or Facebook update I composed.

Every. Single. One.

For years.

Years.

Of course, this was insane and, looking back, I cringe. It's not rational or healthy to need someone's opinion on every "Hi, how are you?" but, at the time, I was so scared to do anything wrong that I wouldn't send a text unless either my mother or father had approved it first. It took me three months to make a simple phone call. Efficiency? Forget it! I couldn't make any decisions myself. *Everything* had to be scrutinized from every angle for weeks on end. I was terrified of making a mistake of any kind because I believed I would lose everything. What I mean is that I felt so much relief in having resurfaced from a psychosis that I didn't want to lose my happiness again. I thought that if I stumbled, people would think of me as an idiot or a weirdo, and my happiness would be in their hands. After so many years of being bullied, other people still had the potential to hurt me. The strange thing is that it didn't matter whether those other people were my friends, family or strangers – I was terrified all the same. Irrational!

I'd hate for others to make the mistakes I did, so if you have schizophrenia and are thinking the same way, listen to me: don't. It's really, truly not worth it. If you get so tied up in knots about what other people think, it will paralyse you, and you will never be able to operate confidently on your own. Think of your life as your story – *you* decide the narrative. Try to understand that writing and sending your own text, email or Facebook post is empowering, not terrifying. Trust your gut feeling about your decisions because the embarrassment of having to ask for a second, third or fourth opinion might end up being more stressful and wearisome than just sending the message! Although I'm much faster nowadays, I can still feel overwhelmed when replying to things because I'm a perfectionist, and my communication must be "just right". Unfortunately, many situations in life require a swift response and, when you have schizophrenia, quickly banging out a reply can *seem* like an impossible hurdle to clamber over.

As mentioned earlier, my mum had to assume many roles during my recovery – including psychologist, nurse, cook, chauffeur, teacher, mentor and many more. Although an open dialogue and lots of communication are vital for recovery, I haven't needed to have a really deep talk for a long time. I used to demand immediate attention, no matter what time of day or night, and conversation that could last for hours, often with no resolution at the end of it. During these talks, I could become angry or upset and lash out at the people who were trying to help me. Or I would sit in near silence, unable to verbalize my thoughts, willing my mum to come up with the answers to what I could not communicate – "mind reader" should be added to her list of responsibilities! The subject would almost always revolve around my difficulties with communication and exasperation that things weren't moving forward fast enough. I am by nature ambitious and driven and have the perpetual feeling that I need to achieve all the time and get ahead in life. This is a core part of my personality and, ironically, part of what has contributed to my recovery, but, on the flip side, if I don't see progress and results, I get really frustrated and need to vent – otherwise, I will explode! These days, I'm getting better at keeping a level head and distracting myself from my angst so that I can see my way forward more clearly and not disturb my parents with *looooooooong* conversations when they are trying to sleep.

At this point, I want to acknowledge my younger brother, Ollie. He has been an absolute saint. A ton of attention has been taken away from him since my breakdown in 2011 – my mum often jokes that he was raised by PlayStation for about three years! He's a wonderful brother: kind, funny, endlessly patient and so watchful and protective of his sister. Schizophrenia is a very demanding illness and requires unlimited resources of time and attention, but he's never complained or made me feel guilty in any way about the amount of attention I require from our parents. It says so much about him and his amazing character. Best. Brother. Ever.

CHAPTER 19
FRIENDS

I have wonderful friends: Miranda ("Mira"), Anna-Cecilie ("AC"), Louise ("Lullo"), Erica ("Eddy"), Marie-Louise ("ML") and Anne Sofie ("Anso"). ML and Anso also happen to be my cousins – so I'm doubly lucky to have them in my life.

(Note: I also have two lovely cousins in Scotland, Ailsa and Rory, but this chapter is about the people around me in my everyday life in Denmark).

We've all known each other since before I became ill – in fact, apart from immediate family, they were the first to realize I wasn't well. For a successful recovery, a strong, supportive network is vital, and I don't want to think about the state I'd be in if I didn't have these women in my life. I wouldn't have come so far in my recovery, that's for sure. Just knowing I have a group of loyal friends is so important to me. Instability of any kind can be poisonous to recovery. In relationships of any kind, stability is key – and my friends deliver! I am forever grateful to them. They know how much they mean to me.

Without friends, you have no one to share fun experiences with, no one to create memories with. Without friends to talk to when things get tough, you won't get the support that's so important when the world seems too much to bear. When you have psychosis, it is important to surround yourself with friends who are caring, patient and trustworthy. Trust is paramount, especially when you have schizophrenia. You can't have anyone gossiping about you behind your back or sharing information about you that you'd rather keep private – how badly would that impact your paranoia?! Schizophrenia can mean that you're not so good at reading social cues or interpreting other people's intentions, and it's possible that you might gravitate toward people that don't have your best interests at heart if you are not careful. "Frienemies" are not something you want in your life!

However, being a good friend *to* your friends can be tough when you have schizophrenia. In the early days after I was discharged from hospital, I barely spoke when I was with my friends. (Note: I hadn't seen them at all during my seven-month hospital stay because visits were limited to close family, so as not to overwhelm me.) When we did eventually meet up, I think my struggle to communicate was very difficult and surprising for them – I'd gone from being relatively animated to completely mute! This is one of the many reasons they're so brilliant for sticking with me all these years. Not many people can cope with someone who is completely mute, especially not as sensitively as my friends have. I felt hopeless and like I had nothing to offer. I was overweight, had no eyebrows due to severe bouts of trichotillomania, and hadn't started my blog, which eventually became my voice. My friends had no idea what was going on in my head, nor who I'd become because of my breakdown, but they were fantastic at allowing me to grow and return to life at my own pace. It took several years, and I cannot overstate how much I appreciate their patience and loyalty. I'm doing so much better now and can talk freely with them with only the occasional blank moment. I really hope that they get as much out of our friendship as I do.

Schizophrenia throws so many obstacles in front of you that being a good friend can sometimes seem impossible, especially when most people don't have the time to invest in someone who doesn't appear to give back. I am extremely reserved in group conversations and don't assert myself at all. An extrovert person, joking around and making people laugh, is bound to earn *waaaaaaaay* more social Brownie points than I ever could. They reap the benefits of their ability to engage so easily with others. Socializing requires a very specific skill set, but with schizophrenia, you may not have the tools required to do the job. So, you just need to find a different set of tools to work with...

In the early days of recovery, it might be better to give yourself some space and time to heal without all kinds of input from others who may or may not be helping you. However, as you get stronger, try your best to nurture existing friendships that feel like they're good for you – and only if you feel that you can. Given that schizophrenics aren't generally good at forward thinking – we can have difficulty with planning ahead – trying to assemble a social life from scratch might be too much of a challenge. And maybe that's okay. Building a network is important but not at the expense of your health. My advice would be to think carefully about your true needs: are you an introvert who loves alone time? Is a lack of a social life distressing you, or are you indifferent? What would your ideal friendships look like, personality-wise? Are you outgoing and able to handle the haphazardness of real-life conversation? Would you feel more comfortable communicating via instant messaging? Could you get what you need from chatting anonymously on online forums?

That was a lot of questions, but they're thoughts I've had, too. To be honest, I've let go of all kinds of ideas that I once held about being social. I thought I had to be out there, that I could only be accepted and considered normal by being social and getting lots of invitations to parties. Eventually, I phased these thoughts out because I realized they were cluttering up my mind and causing major FOMO – fear of missing out. As it turns out, I'm happy with my network as it is: my family and small circle of close friends enrich my life so much that I don't need anything more than that.

I've come a long way in my recovery thanks to my friends, but I also know that, during this time, my social life has depended on *them* being proactive about arranging coffee, lunch, etc. In the early days of my recovery, I was not so good at arranging things, much as I would have liked to, so I had to rely on my friends taking the lead. That said, I am getting much better at initiating contact and am quite the social butterfly these days, all things considered.

If you have good friends that have stayed in your life for better and for worse, that is truly a gift, but don't stress yourself by thinking you have to be a certain way socially or have X number of friends. Forcing things never feels right, and maybe you're exactly where you're meant to be. I hope you can find the right balance for you. It's your life. It's your recovery. Give yourself time and respect your own process.

CHAPTER 20
ROMANTIC RELATIONSHIPS

SIGH.

Love makes the world go round! Romantic relationships: the conflicts, mixed messages, rejections and heartbreaks, not to mention the expectation of fairy-tale endings − or the hard reality of making it work!

There are many types of relationships and many expectations surrounding them. Taylor Swift sings about them all the time, and romantic comedies are filled with the boy-meets-girl, boy-loses-girl, boy-gets-girl-back, boy-and-girl-live-happily-ever-after formula. In real life, love's not just about holding hands and walking on the beach − it's a lot of hard work and compromise, compromise, compromise. When I was younger, I had a rather idealistic view of what being in a relationship meant, but I think I'm a little more realistic now.

I've never had a boyfriend. That's not to say I've never been on dates − I have. I've been rejected and I've rejected others. I was hurt by the former, and I still feel bad about the latter.

However, knowing what I now know about my illness and how it affects me, perhaps it's for the best that I've never been seriously involved with anyone. Painful and frustrating as it's been, I realize that I am too fragile to cope with the ups and downs of my own life, let alone be involved in someone else's! That's not to say that others with schizophrenia cannot have successful long-term romantic relationships – I'm just discussing it from my personal viewpoint.

You see, what it all boils down to is STRESS – positive and negative – and I'll come back to that in a second.

Getting a boyfriend, in very basic terms, requires being out there socially, and that's where I fall short. Too much pressure. Due to my illness, my brain is simply not programmed to play the games people play when trying to attract and keep a mate – it's a foreign language to me. (David Attenborough should do a special on the non-existent mating rituals of the paranoid schizophrenic… #joke.) Of course, I don't speak for everyone – but, in my case, I am just not equipped to play the dating game. Besides, what I've got to offer isn't exactly a bowl of honey for prospective dates: "Hello, here I am with my chronic brain disease that has wiped my communication hard drive, meaning *you'll* have to make all the effort in getting to know me. And, even though I'm a lovely person – honest! – I don't possess a good memory, long-term concentration, forward-planning skills, normal attention span or the ability to read and understand body language. Oh, and I don't speak very much."

What a dream date! I can just see them all now, lined up around the block… *not.*

For me, the process of finding and keeping a partner is like crossing a minefield in snowshoes. It requires an advanced skill set to be attentive, empathetic, sexy, humorous, affectionate, communicative, cheerful, fun to be around, interesting, spontaneous, conversational and, if possible, to look nice too. It would help me to have a life outside this relationship and to be able to socialize with their friends too (*brain explodes*). On top of that, I must have the courage to invite them into my life… and expose my vulnerabilities.

Yikes!

I have a hard enough time caring for myself. How would I find the energy to do so sufficiently for someone else? *Sooooooo* much stress!

Stress – negative or positive – is the mortal enemy of a successful recovery and certainly doesn't help when it comes to forming romantic relationships. Negative stress is associated with feeling like you're failing, you're falling behind or not living up to certain expectations. Positive stress, the less-understood kind, is connected to emotions like excitement and anticipation. Both kinds of stress are very much present in the process of committing to someone – from the first fluttery feelings of "do they/don't they?" to declaring your relationship on social media.

So, I'm in a bit of a Catch-22 situation: being in a relationship with someone could be detrimental to my health, but I can't control what my heart feels. On the other hand, I have many wonderful qualities – so I'm told! – but how is any potential partner going to see them if I can't express myself due to the limitations caused by my illness?

Sometimes, I long to be a "normal" young woman, able to chat easily and feel comfortable socially. It would be lovely to have the same starting point as everyone else when it comes to dating but, unfortunately, it's not a level playing field when you're trying to navigate through life with a faulty compass.

Oooh, that got a bit deep, didn't it?!

A lot of what you have just read is based on the way I felt back in 2018, when my first book was published in Denmark, and I was beginning to find my voice again. I'd been hoping with each year that passed that romance would happen for me, that I'd finally find a partner to share my life with, bring to family get-togethers – someone who'd appreciate me for me. I wouldn't say I felt incomplete without a boyfriend, but I did envy my friends' ability to find a partner with relative ease. Why couldn't I do the same? Was I undesirable? Incompetent? Boring? What? I wasn't ugly. I wasn't smelly. I didn't wear outrageous outfits. Was I trying too hard? Maybe I was trying too *little*? As you can probably tell, I analysed it into oblivion, but never found the answers. I couldn't understand why, as a nice-looking, friendly, intelligent person, I wasn't getting the same kind of attention as my contemporaries. Eventually, I guess there just came a point where I had enough. I was sick of feeling ignored and unwanted, however true or untrue those assumptions may have been. Why bother to get so invested? Nowadays, instead of looking for love, I'm looking to build a three-dimensional and fulfilling life. I work on myself, my art and my writing and try to do what is best for me. I adhere to the principle that, if someone's interested, hopefully they'll make the effort to get to know me better – and, if it's mutual, that would be great. Otherwise, I've resolved to stay single for now. I'm happy this way and I've realized that my worth is not defined by whether or not I'm in a romantic relationship.

I hope this sheds some light on what it's like to contemplate relationships when you have schizophrenia. Of course, everyone's experience is different, so I'm not saying that this is true for everyone – it is just how it's been for me and, perhaps, someone else can relate to it too.

REMINDER: it is important to understand that, in schizophrenia, stress is detrimental to recovery – and both negative and positive stress need to be managed very carefully.

QUICK QUESTION:

What do you think is the biggest misconception about people with schizophrenia?

That we're all violent, dangerous and out of control. I once saw someone (in a Facebook comment) describe schizophrenics as "ticking time bombs". That stuck with me.

CHAPTER 21
DISCLOSURE

Deciding to go public with my diagnosis was not a quick and easy decision – but it was a good one.

Initially, because I wanted to keep my diagnosis private until I had come to terms with it, my family told anyone who asked that "Georgia has some problems with stress," and that was the reason I'd dropped out of gymnasium and was seeing a psychiatrist. I wasn't ready to tell the world about my new label and, naturally, my family wanted to protect me. I worried that people might judge me negatively or simply distance themselves from me if they knew the truth. I eventually told my closest friends – because they asked – and I trusted that they would keep my "secret". For a few years, this strategy seemed to work, and I felt safer keeping my diagnosis private.

Then, in 2015, I suffered a relapse – it was sudden and horrible, and it took six months to get back on my feet again. It came as a shock to all of us because I had been doing so well up to that point.

It was after this that we chose to go public with my diagnosis. It wasn't an immediate decision, but one that came about after a lot of discussion and reassurance that I was happy with that choice. After my relapse, my mum reasoned that, although my schizophrenia didn't define me, it *was* a part of me and something that wasn't going to just disappear. She felt that it would better for me and the family to be open about it. She told me, "Most people are very kind, Georgia, and they will not think any less of you for being open about your diagnosis – in fact, I think they will applaud your bravery. If anyone is mean-spirited or cruel about it, then they are not a friend and certainly have no place in your life going forward. I think it will lift a heavy weight off all our shoulders because it has been incredibly stressful for you – and us – to 'lie' to our friends and colleagues about what's really going on. I truly believe that honesty and openness are the best policy for you and that you will be happy with your decision to go public. In fact, I think it will be a relief. However, you need to understand that, once it is out of the bag, there is no putting it back in there. Schizophrenia is still a much-misunderstood illness – with all the stigma that goes with that ignorance – so you must be comfortable with any decision that we make."

She's a wise owl, my mum.

However, I wasn't just going to sling out my diagnosis in conversation. I needed to tell people in a controlled, careful way. I knew I wasn't strong verbally so, for me, putting it in writing was the way forward. With the help of my parents, I started sending emails out to my friends telling the truth.

When we went to social arrangements, we began explaining to friends that I had schizophrenia, what it was and how it affected me. My parents and I were determined to try to demystify the illness, and they encouraged people to ask questions and to feel comfortable around the subject.

I was blown away by the response.

Everyone was so unfazed, kind and accommodating. They asked questions and showed genuine interest in my diagnosis and its challenges, which I did my best to answer as clearly as possible in spite of my cognitive symptoms and other communication barriers. If I got stuck, my parents would step in and explain on my behalf. I began to wonder why I'd waited so long to tell people – that was how positive the response was.

I started my Danish blog a year later. On my blog, I could express myself fully – my own way, my own words, my own terms. It was perfect. Instead of having to tell every single person I knew separately, I could communicate in writing to a wide audience, sharing everything I needed to say, which was incredibly therapeutic for me and would help me to finally feel in control of my situation.

This didn't mean I wasn't ambivalent about going public. In fact, I was terrified every time I hit publish on a blog post. (The first time I posted, I was shaking so much that I could barely hit the right key!) But, with time, it got easier, and the positive feedback I received helped enormously. I felt fired up and motivated to share my story.

CHAPTER 22
AVOIDING RELAPSE

On 1 January 2015, I had a relapse.

It was as if someone had flicked a switch and turned me off. Sudden, unexpected and dark. None of us saw it coming.

I had to take a time-out from life for several months. Four months passed before I felt able to go to ceramics and see my friends again (and even that was pushing it). It would take a full year to feel like I had returned to firing on all cylinders. I took an increased dose of my medicine every day and my psychiatric nurse, E, was available for regular talks and advice, which was a brilliant help in my recovery.

In the early stages of the relapse, I isolated myself in my room, doing nothing other than surfing the web and occasionally writing. I was moody, withdrawn and barely spoke. I avoided eye contact and had very little energy. I wasn't aware of how bad my decline was until I was out of it again. When I was in it, all I could do was protect myself from too much input and allow myself to recover at my own pace.

My advice to anyone coming out of relapse would be to take it slowly. Don't rush things. Don't push yourself to do more than you feel capable of. I say this because, five months after I relapsed, I arranged to go out with a guy on a walk, thinking I could manage it. As it so happened, when the day came, I couldn't say a word. Not one. I think I managed to answer his questions, when asked, but my brain was still so frazzled that I was unable to think of anything to say. If the poor guy hadn't kept asking me questions, we'd have walked around in absolute silence. Needless to say, after that disaster, he wasn't interested in going on another walk. And who can blame him?

Disaster is, of course, an exaggeration – but it was certainly a wake-up call. I realized that, even if I felt okay, I probably needed some more time to recover and regain my conversational skills!

I can't change what happened and I wouldn't change what happened – it was a lesson learned. However, I hope to provide some guidance to anyone in the same situation. If you don't respect your own boundaries, you risk falling into ill health again – or simply making a mess of a situation that could've been completely "normal"!

I know it's not easy, and avoiding situations like that will sometimes be impossible. In that case, my best advice would be to plan all you can beforehand: write conversation topics down in your phone; prepare yourself for awkward silences and how you will handle them; try to visualize yourself in the situation from the outside and the image you want to convey; focus on what you're thinking and feeling – can you translate that into conversation? Be as honest as possible. If you're feeling shy or nervous, say so. If you can't think of anything to say, laugh and say, "Sorry, I've gone more blank than the answers section in my physics exam!" Anything that will ease the situation for you and the other person involved. Ask questions if you find that easier than talking about yourself. If the other person is asking you questions, flesh out your answers a bit rather than just saying "yes" or "no". You don't have to divulge your whole life story, but giving them a bit of insight into who you are will make you seem open and genuine. I've learned the hard way that being too inhibited confuses people and makes them wonder what you're hiding, which can put them off if they feel they've opened up a lot to you.

We all know that conversation is a give-and-take – but it can be extremely difficult for someone suffering from schizophrenia. Planning ahead is a good trick if you can manage it. I wish I'd thought about that before I completely messed up my potential date with a nice guy – but that's just the way it is. And it's okay.

So, how does one avoid relapse?

The best thing you can do is to keep taking your medicine, talking things through with your psychiatrist, seeking support from your network and trying to maintain your everyday routines. As I learned, relapse can come like a bolt from the blue if you're not paying close attention to your symptoms. Given that anyone can slip up, perhaps it's not feasible to guarantee that you'll never relapse again. However, if you adhere to your treatment and keep yourself active within what you can handle (mentally, socially, practically, etc.), that should hopefully keep true disaster at bay.

CHAPTER 23
STIGMA AND TABOO

As I'm writing this chapter, it is Mental Health Awareness Week: a vital campaign for breaking down the stigma attached to mental illnesses. Unfortunately, schizophrenia is often inaccurately portrayed by the media, due to their penchant for highlighting the more sensational stories related to the small percentage of sufferers who are involved in crime. However, it should be understood this represents a minority of people living with schizophrenia. Violence is not a symptom of the disease.

I hope my story can help break down some of the many myths and misconceptions surrounding schizophrenia and encourage open dialogue about mental illness in general. It is unfair that sufferers should have the added burden of marginalization from society, due to uninformed public opinion. Isn't having schizophrenia enough in itself?

So, what can be done about the misunderstandings that surround schizophrenia? Well, talking about your own experience of mental illness is an excellent start. However, the subject needs to be handled carefully. Before disclosing your diagnosis to someone, you have to think about several things: do I trust this person? Is it necessary to tell them? When do I tell them? How are they likely to react? Am I comfortable with them knowing it – forever? Can I count on them keeping it to themselves (or is that not an issue for me)? Will they appreciate me telling them about my diagnosis and support me, or will they distance themselves from me?

To be honest, you can never know exactly how a person will react – and sometimes people's responses may surprise you (one way or another). Personally, I found that being honest and open about my diagnosis was a massive relief for me and my family. My close friends all knew from the start because, as soon as I was discharged from hospital, they were curious to know what had happened. As it is, everyone I told has been inordinately kind and supportive – even grateful – that I've confided in them. It was an eye-opener for me to see that I wasn't being judged negatively – I think I've actually become even closer to my friends because of how we all handled the situation. In fact, the positive reactions I received encouraged me to create my first blog in 2016.

However, my experience doesn't mean that your situation will be exactly the same, so it's important to consider your audience before opening up about your diagnosis. Sadly, there is still a great deal of misunderstanding surrounding schizophrenia, so whoever you're telling might not know how to react, and you might not be equipped to handle this. It's best to prepare how to tell people in advance, rather than just blurting it out. Of course, there are situations in which you may have to inform people – perhaps your colleagues are concerned about your long absence from work – and it may cause further complications if you avoid the subject, rather than just explaining that you had a relapse. Depending on the situation, maybe you could write them an email instead. This gives you time to craft a well-thought-out piece, rather than stuttering and getting flustered while trying to think out something relevant on the spot.

In general, listen to your intuition and have a plan. Make use of the written word if talking about it will be too stressful. Also, when you do decide to tell people, try to keep it as light, informative and relatable as possible. For example, test the waters by telling them you had a breakdown and had to go to hospital for a while. If they seem curious and ask you about it, you can say you were diagnosed with schizophrenia. Gauge their reaction, and if they're like, "Oh!" and seem a little thrown by the information, don't panic – they might not know what the correct response is and may be worried about saying the wrong thing. Perhaps this is your cue to tell them that you are happy to answer any questions they may have about it – or put it down in an email for them to read at their leisure.

If they are more open to talking about it, you can start by explaining what it is and isn't. That it is a brain disease, like Alzheimer's or Parkinson's, and that you're not violent or dangerous, as movies, newspapers and general ignorance are prone to imply. You can discuss how you struggle with things like concentration, conversation, forward-planning and memory tasks – and how you can become easily overwhelmed by things that other people would consider minor. If they ask more questions, you could mention that you hear voices and describe other more personal aspects of the illness. You can also make it clear to them that you're not going to appear demon-like in their bedroom mirror at midnight – a little humour can go a long way when introducing people to schizophrenia! I've found that by highlighting the more relatable aspects of schizophrenia first – the things people might be able to apply to themselves or, at the very least, sympathize with – it makes people more relaxed and likely to feel empathy toward you.

To go back to the subject of stigma and taboo, perhaps you might feel able to volunteer for a mental health organization or start your own blog about your experiences with mental illness. There are many ways of raising awareness about schizophrenia and other mental illnesses, but don't feel any pressure to do it if you don't feel up for it. I started my blog for many reasons, including an overwhelming need to express myself. I also realized, "I will never be able to tell all these people my diagnosis one by one – but, perhaps, if I write about it…?" Bingo! I post whenever I have something to say, which can be weekly or once every couple of months. Writing helps me, and I've found it helps others too, so I have the motivation to do it. However, exposing myself in this way can sometimes feel overwhelming, so I periodically take a break from blogging to give myself a little time to recoup. Do whatever you need to do – at your own pace – and look after yourself.

Let's make it taboo to *ignore* mental illness – rather than taboo to *talk about it.*

CHAPTER 24
SUICIDE AND PSYCHOSIS

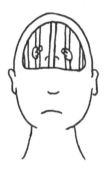

We recently lost a family friend to suicide. It's a tragedy that reminds us how someone's personal demons can be so unbearable that they can see no other way out.

The rule of quarters, which I describe in the next chapter, suggests that approximately 10 per cent of schizophrenics die by suicide. Compared to the general population, it is a considerably higher percentage among those suffering from schizophrenia and should not be ignored.

Many years ago, during a school class, I drew a girl holding a gun on one of my notebooks. It was just a doodle, inspired by the murder-mystery manga books that I enjoy, and it was drawn with no intention to cause concern. However, the boy sitting next to me said, "Wow, Georgia, that's kind of dark, isn't it?!" In retrospect, I am a little embarrassed about it because I really didn't mean to freak him out. However, though I've never been suicidal, ANY indication of suicidal thinking or behaviour – including drawing something "dark" in a schoolbook – should always be taken very seriously. It is a myth that, if someone talks about suicide, they won't actually do it. If someone talks about it – listen – and take it very seriously indeed. Talk to them: ask them if they are having thoughts of harming themselves; be alert for warning signs – listen to what they are not saying; ask if there is a trusted person you could talk to on their behalf; suggest going to the doctor with them; keep the dialogue open; keep them company; keep them in your sights. Tell someone if you are at all concerned.

There is a saying, "Suicide is a long-term solution to a short-term problem," but, in reality, this is too glib a slogan for such a complex subject. For some people, their demons are *not* a short-term problem, but a persistent and never-ending form of torture, and suicide might be the only way to end their agony. I've never been suicidal and do not feel qualified to talk about it, but I have seen the devastating impact it has on the people left behind and know that it should always be taken seriously. If you or anyone you know is talking about ending their life, do not be afraid to step in and get them the help and support that they need.

QUICK QUESTION:

What's the biggest taboo you'd like to break down with your book about schizophrenia?

I'd like to show the world that we are perfectly normal, able members of society, even if our level of functioning is a little different from other people's.

We're not scary creatures to be locked away in a dungeon and kept from the rest of society.

I hope to bridge the gap between "neurotypicals" and "society's weakest members".

CHAPTER 25
PROGNOSIS

When you have schizophrenia, there are four groups that can predict the outcome of your recovery. This is known as the rule of quarters (and replaces the previous rule of thirds that was applied before improvements in treatment and medicine).

The rule of quarters

According to this rule, 25 per cent of those diagnosed with schizophrenia will recover fully and experience no further problems. Twenty-five per cent will improve significantly with treatment, regaining (almost) their prior level of functioning and have very few relapses. Twenty-five per cent will improve a little, but still require a significant amount of support to function normally and may expect a number of relapses. Of the remaining 25 per cent, 15 per cent won't improve much and will stay in hospital for most of their lives, and the final 10 per cent will, most likely, die – often by suicide.

Before I had my relapse in 2015, I had assumed I'd be in the first group because I had been doing so well in my recovery. However, I am now not sure what group I belong to. Perhaps I should create my own: a fifth group that – fingers crossed – won't relapse again and surpasses their previous level of functioning – hurrah! Admittedly, I still require a lot of support and reassurance, but I always try to look on the positive side of life.

I can only speak for myself, but I've come to terms with the fact that there are certain things that I will never be able to do.

Driving

My brain is simply not capable of handling so many impressions at once – traffic, road signs, lights, crossings, pedestrians, bikes, other drivers – and if you aren't super alert while driving, you shouldn't be on the road. There are also too many things for me to remember behind the wheel, and the possibility of unexpected events that require fast decisions would completely panic me – and a moving car isn't exactly the best place to have a meltdown. I live in a fairly small town and can go everywhere on foot, so being able to drive is not a big loss for me. I know there are many people with schizophrenia who can drive and have no issues with it – but how on earth do *you* manage with all those impressions and things to remember? I am impressed!

Supermarket shopping

If I could go food shopping, I would. I really hate feeling pathetic, and I can hear some of you shouting, "Don't be such a wimp!" But as soon as I enter a supermarket, I'm completely overwhelmed by all the impressions: so much stuff to look at, so many people to avoid, so many decisions to be made! My brain freezes, my ambivalence takes over, and I can't decide which jam I should buy from the 20-plus kinds on display. I usually give up and leave the shop, feeling like an absolute failure and so downhearted that I can't do something as simple as buying food! Luckily, online supermarkets mean that I can order what I need, at my own pace in my own home, and it gets delivered right to my door. Perfect.

Cooking

I've never been able to cook, despite my Danish grandfather's best efforts to get me interested. My brain is not geared to multitasking, and I can't seem to coordinate all the things required to put a meal together. I also have an irrational fear of the oven – crazy, huh? – and my paranoia about food dates and food poisoning means that I worry so much about things being cooked correctly that I end up not being able to eat them. Add to that not possessing the organizational abilities needed to follow cookbook instructions, and I am truly a recipe for disaster in the kitchen – did you see what I did there? I can just about manage to heat things up on a hob, but cooking a meal from scratch and using that big, scary, hot oven are out of the question.

Getting an education and job

On a more serious note, two major choices that I've had to come to terms with are not being able to study or hold down a job. This has frustrated me enormously. I did try to return to education after my breakdown but, as I discussed previously, it was too much for me because my voices multiplied and I couldn't interact with groups of people I didn't know. I also worked in a friend's publishing house for a while, but, again, it proved to be too much for me when I couldn't follow simple instructions, speak up or contribute. For a long time, I thought, if I couldn't do these things, then what was the point to anything? What was the point of me? How would I stimulate my brain? How would I stave off boredom? How could I ever be a productive member of society? It took several years, and many more attempts at education and working, for me to realize that I needed to find a different way to use my brain to contribute. Eventually, I found it through writing, art and ceramics. I know that in other circumstances

I could have gained great academic qualifications – prior to my breakdown, I was a straight-A student – and may have made a valuable contribution in the workplace. I have had to make my peace with that.

Getting married and having children

I don't want kids. Never have. From an early age, I've known that I wanted to focus on a career rather than having a family, and my diagnosis confirmed my decision. Again, I can only speak from my perspective – and I'm fully aware that there are many people with schizophrenia who are successfully raising families – but I am certain that I would be incapable of carrying, taking care of and raising a child. A child needs constant care and attention, but I need to take a time out for several days after any kind of social arrangement; how would I ever be able to cope with the demands of a baby? I can't just put it back if I'm tired! What about pregnancy and hormonal chaos and the possible implications of being on antipsychotics? The organizational skills required to be a mother are beyond my abilities. And, if you remember, I am frightened of ovens and paranoid about best-before dates – so mealtimes would be, er, interesting, to say the least! For me, there are too many things at stake and I'm not willing to risk my health or jeopardize the well-being of a baby. I also worry about the genetic possibility of passing my illness on to my child. Luckily, I had made up my mind about motherhood long before the paranoid schizophrenia kicked in, but I know that there are many women and men out there for whom parenthood is a longed-for dimension to their life. I respect their choices and understand that it is not an easy decision either way.

(P.S. Nine months of gaining weight, throwing up and then screaming in agony while trying to squeeze the equivalent of a watermelon through a straw doesn't exactly appeal either. Yikes!)

* * *

I think it's safe to say that, according to society's standards, I might not qualify as a prime example of normal. My skills and capabilities are very specific. I have a high IQ but often can't figure out how to pull blinds down. I can draw a portrait of Adele that makes people go, "Wow!" but cannot remember how to work a tumble dryer without a how-to note stuck to the machine.

I guess one can't have it all!

How would you define a good prognosis? What does recovery mean to you?

To me, recovery means constantly moving forward – at a pace and in a way that makes sense to me. In this regard, I think it's imperative to have goals to work toward; to have that carrot, that sense of purpose and a reason to get up in the morning. When you've had a psychosis or any other kind of breakdown, your life has been shattered into a million tiny pieces and things can seem hopeless. Perhaps you feel that trying is pointless, but it isn't. Sometimes, for me, just getting up in the morning *is* the motivation. On other occasions, the main purpose of my day is just to *be*, not to *do*. Maybe this contradicts what I said before, but we can't have productive days all the time, nor can we be on all the time. So, especially in the initial stages of your recovery, take it easy and don't risk a relapse by trying to achieve more than you are capable of at the time. It was only many years after my breakdown that I began to aim for more, and I wouldn't have been able to do that had I not seriously respected my personal limitations in the beginning.

Ultimately, *my* motivation is writing. It always has been. I'm driven to do it. However, when I was in hospital, I didn't write creatively at all – at least not for the first six months. It was only toward the end of my hospitalization that I tentatively took out my pen and big yellow notebook and wrote a few sentences. Even then, I felt very uninspired. My brain just wasn't in it, which was completely understandable, given the magnitude of my breakdown.

For me, even if I only manage to write four lines of poetry in one day, that's still progress. It's still worth something. It doesn't even need to be something as concrete as that. Rearranging your brain takes time – lots of time. Not all headway can be measured in tangible, visible results. Your progress could be that you've managed to overcome an internal barrier, such as being able to shrug and say "never mind", rather than feeling devastated about the outcome of a small setback in your life. It could be saying "no" to something because saying no is best for you, when, before, you might have said "yes" just to please someone. It might be feeling more confident about your own abilities, even without having to prove it to anyone. Often, the biggest epiphanies and changes don't require shouting from the rooftops. Pay attention to what makes you feel better and follow your intuition.

It's not necessarily the big leaps and bounds, but the small steps you implement every day that mean the most. You can't eat an elephant in one bite. It's the same with introducing good habits into your life that will carry you toward your goals: you have to take them one step at a time, however frustrating that may seem. I know how exasperated the competitive side of me gets when I'm told to have patience, but I need to listen... because it works!

Writing a book didn't happen overnight. Prior to my first book being published, I wrote several blog posts over the course of two years before a publisher contacted me and suggested my words and illustrations would work very well as a book. With the book you're reading now, I had to do masses of rearranging my brain to sit down and write it. It took an enormous amount of time and mental and physical energy to complete it. But I am so glad that I persevered and hope that you are enjoying it.

So, what I've done might not be for everyone. Writing takes a lot of effort. It can be tedious and frustrating when you know what you want to say but cannot find the right words. Contacting a publisher takes a lot of time and energy and is also a very scary part of the process – putting yourself out there to be exposed and judged by strangers! Waiting for a response tests your nerves. Receiving a rejection is disheartening when you've invested months of your time and all your passion into your manuscript. And this is before your book is even on the shelf and subject to the scrutiny of the general public. Although it is an exhausting process for me, I accept it because writing is my lifeline, my way to communicate and, hopefully, a means to help other people.

I'm still not entirely certain about my prognosis and what the future holds for me. Will I end up recovering fully? What would a full recovery even look like? All I can do is live my life the best way that I can, take my medicine, listen to the medical experts and my family, and do what works for me. Perhaps if you do the same, you'll find your voice too.

CHAPTER 26
PUNCTUALITY

After experiencing psychosis, a life skill that can be difficult to reacquire is punctuality. It's generally accepted that being late to appointments demonstrates a lack of respect for other people's time and is not acceptable in today's competitive society, especially in the job market. On a personal level, even good friends will tire of you if you're always making them wait.

However, with schizophrenia, it's not easy to live up to expectations of punctuality. I know from my own experience that I don't possess a sense of urgency and this, combined with ambivalence and voices, makes things more complicated. Ambivalence makes you question everything, and voices make you question your own questions! Although I do my best to be on time and keep myself as calm as possible about it – because, once stressed, I freeze up and can't do anything – this combination of factors can be a recipe for tardi–saster. See what I did there?

When I know I'm going to be late for a social appointment, I send a brief, apologetic text indicating when I expect to arrive to let my friend know that I am okay, just delayed. On arrival, I apologize again, explain my reasons and hope that they understand. This strategy – and the patience of my friends! – is helpful to me in two ways. Firstly, I acknowledge my lateness to them and to myself, in the hope that I will learn to be more punctual next time. And secondly, I gain the breathing space I need to avoid completely freaking out because I am running late. I know this is standard behaviour for anyone who is running late, but, for me, it is learned behaviour that I use to keep myself calm when trying to stay connected to people.

I *hate* being late – it really stresses me. I used to be late for everything: school, dentist appointments, friends. I knew I had to fix the problem, but I struggled with it. Life moved too fast for me, and I found it hard to understand the concept of urgency. Now, I'm much more able to show up on time – even early – and, amazingly, my friends now see me as a punctual person. I think I have been greatly helped by a less frenetic schedule. I no longer have to fit into the demands of a school or work timetable, nor use rush-hour public transport, and, as a result, my time-keeping has improved. I now have the space to focus on improving my punctuality because my lifestyle is more structured and manageable for me.

I know how important it is to not waste other people's time, and my phone is a useful tool to help me with this. I make good use of the phone's electronic reminders to keep me alert to anything I must do during the day. It's vital for me to plan what I need to do to ensure that I don't lose track of time and freeze up in panic, something I've often experienced in the past. It's horrible: I *know* what I have to do, but as soon as I see I'm going to be late, I can't move. I feel so angry with myself and the situation and just want to crawl back under my duvet and ignore the world for the rest of the day. Obviously, this is not a great strategy, so if you ever feel this way, try to get through it – though I know it's challenging when the feeling has already planted itself.

Anyway, that is my take on punctuality. Now, if anyone could give *me* some advice on how to actually *hear* your alarm and get up without snoozing it, that would be lovely…!

CHAPTER 27
A "TRICHY" SITUATION

And now for something that I haven't discussed publicly – ever.

Alongside my schizophrenia, I suffer from trichotillomania.

Trich, as it's called for short, is a compulsive disorder which causes you to pull out your own hair. Sufferers feel an overwhelming urge to pull eyelashes, eyebrows, head hair or strands anywhere else on their bodies. In my case, I have only pulled my eyelashes and eyebrows. The compulsion often begins in childhood. I was nine years old when I first started pulling and twelve by the time it had become so obvious that my mum asked me, "Are you missing some eyelashes?"

Often, but not always, a pulling session starts with a tingling sensation in the area from which you normally pull. Pulling can be conscious or unconscious, and the reward is a sense of relief. Unfortunately, like many compulsive behaviours, the relief is short-lived and is promptly replaced by the urge to pull again. I frequently get the urge to pull when I'm zoning out in front of the computer, reading something or about to fall asleep. I never pull in the company of other people.

Trichotillomania makes you feel so ashamed. Who wants to admit that they deliberately pull out their own hair?! For this reason, many sufferers go to great lengths to cover up the damage. For years I've used eyebrow pencil, eyeliner and, when possible, mascara. At one point, I barely had any eyelashes at all and had to start buying the most realistic fake lashes I could find. Other sufferers might resort to wearing wigs to conceal the bald spots on their heads or make excuses about their condition, telling people that they suffer from alopecia, a seemingly more acceptable reason for hair loss than trichotillomania. It makes you feel awful about yourself – you feel like a freak, and you're far too ashamed to tell anyone. Trichotillomania is a relatively unknown disorder – in my experience, there is not much advice or help to be found – which is compounded by the fact that most people won't admit they suffer from it, as they are so mortified by their behaviour. It's a vicious cycle of shame.

I suspect my friends have figured it out about me because there's only so much I can do to hide it. It's not a disorder that one can keep undercover because it directly impacts one's appearance, which makes it even more devastating when I find myself unable to control it.

Trich is psychological agony – it ruins the sufferer's looks and self-esteem. Even though I say to myself, "I *hate* the consequences of this," it is almost impossible to stop once the urge sets in. I have tried all kinds of things to stop myself: stress balls, origami, gloves, Vaseline on my brows or lashes to make them too slippery to pull, and a rubber band around my wrist to snap against the skin when I get the urge. However, for me, they are temporary solutions that don't seem to help the long-term behaviour. When the urge is strong enough, nothing can stop it. There are indications that Cognitive Behavioural Therapy (CBT) has proven successful for some for sufferers, and I have been looking into that as a possible solution for me.

Currently, my eyebrows are in relatively good shape because I have been more in control lately. However, I have been pulling for 18 years, which may have caused irreparable damage to the hair follicles.

I will be devastated if my brows can't grow back fully, and it is hugely frustrating that I struggle to fight a strong compulsion to pull. What seems to work for me is visualizing myself *with* brows and imagining the effect that will have on my self-confidence: a kind of positive reinforcement therapy for my face! On my phone, I keep old photos of myself with full brows, as well as pictures of celebrities such as Lily Collins, Jennifer Connelly and Billie Eilish, who all have *gorgeous* eyebrows. This helps motivate me. I've tried tracking my progress with a habit-tracking app, which proved useful for a while, but the real change has been made by trying to readjust my way of thinking and visualizing myself with full brows. I no longer beat myself up if I end up pulling a few hairs because, as much as I want full brows back, I don't want to hate myself in the process. I have considered the option of microblading and might go down that road in the future.

This is an incredibly sensitive and embarrassing topic for me because I have spent most of my life feeling so ashamed about it. I really had to think long and hard about including it in this book. I hope, by being open about it, I might help someone like me. It's difficult to know what to say, especially with such an emotive and personal subject, but if I've helped someone to feel that they're not alone, shown them that their disorder has a name, or shared some tips they can use in their own "kick-the-trich" process, that would make me happy. It helps me so much to write about things like this, so it's a wonderful bonus if others benefit from it, too.

CHAPTER 28
DEPRESSION IN SCHIZOPHRENIA

Until the end of 2020, I'd never considered myself a depressed person. Then, in December, I received a diagnosis of depression.

I had been struggling, without really realizing it, in the preceding months. My mum spotted the changes in my mood: crying a lot more than I normally did – particularly late at night – and talking about how I felt like the walls were "closing in on me". I felt as if I would never achieve even half of what I wanted in my life, and that distressed me. So, my mum suggested that I write everything down so I'd have something to show my doctor in case my mind went blank in his surgery, and we made an appointment to see him as soon as possible. After the doctor read my notes – and had a long talk with me – he diagnosed me with mild depression. I should state here that my doctor has been with me since before my schizophrenia diagnosis. It was him who was the first to understand that there was something seriously wrong with me, and he got me the help I needed, so he has a particularly good understanding of my health situation. He is also a personal friend of our family and, due to that, has a three-dimensional understanding of me: medically, socially and personally. He is fantastic and has been an incredible support and help to me and my family through everything. We owe him a huge debt of gratitude.

The depression diagnosis came as a surprise to me. I'm generally a happy, positive person with an optimistic approach to life, so I assumed I'd managed to avoid boarding the depression train. Depression in schizophrenia is fairly common, though. There are several reasons for this, including the loneliness and despair that accompany the disruption caused by psychosis. When you're a young adult and psychosis comes along and destroys all your plans, who can blame you for falling into a dark place? Plus, there's the pain of isolation that comes from being out of work, living alone, having poor communication skills, etc. Schizophrenia is such a brutally unfair disease in so many ways, and it seems particularly cruel that one should have to deal with depression on top of everything else.

I take sertraline for my depression, which has proven very effective for me. It usually takes about six weeks for the medicine to take effect, which feels like a lifetime when you're struggling. After that, the medicine proved effective at lifting my mood and clearing the grey clouds that were hovering above my head. I have also realized that sunny weather greatly improves my mood. Seasonal affective disorder (SAD) is common among many people and can be eased during the darker months with the use of a daylight lamp, some of which are about the size of an iPad and very portable. Regular sessions with my GP and psychiatrist have also been of great help.

There is a difference between having a short-term episode of depression and major depressive disorder, and this fact was vital for me to hold on to during my recovery process. I am a cheerful and optimistic person – these are some of my favourite qualities about myself – and I couldn't bear to lose those qualities. If I am being honest, I think that having depression felt like a failure on my part, which I know is such a ridiculous way to think about it. Of course, now that I am feeling much better, I can see that it was in no way a failure, but just another hurdle to be climbed over on my path to recovery.

(Note: I listened to a lot of music in the weeks after my depression diagnosis – "Clocks" by Coldplay and "Elastic Heart" by Sia were particularly therapeutic, as was *Confessions on a Dance Floor* by Madonna. There's certain music I must be in the mood for, and they all hit the spot at the time. Thank you, music!)

COPING STRATEGIES – VOICES

How to cope with voices:

1. **Take the medicine.** It won't work immediately, and you may have to try different types and combinations before you find the one that works for you, but it is so important to stick with it. Medicine can relieve unpleasant symptoms, including voices. Antipsychotics work on a long-term basis and, if you suddenly stop taking them without consulting your doctor or psychiatrist, you risk relapse. Even when you feel an improvement in your symptoms, keep taking your medicine and listen to your doctor's advice – they are the ones who can safely evaluate whether you should reduce or increase your medication. It is also important to understand that successful treatment is an ongoing process that can take many years. If you experience unpleasant side effects, speak to your psychiatrist about them, as they are usually resolvable.
2. **Keep track of your voices.** You don't have to do this all the time – sometimes, just a few sessions are enough to make you see your voices in a different light. For me, writing down what my voices say helps me to understand how stupid their comments or demands are. When I hear them in my head, they appear to make sense, but on paper, they just look silly! For example, when they say, "She's brushing her teeth like a maniac," I will immediately feel self-conscious. But once I see it written down, I question how someone can brush their teeth "like a maniac"?! No matter how I try, I can't connect it to the girl in the mirror, who is brushing her teeth perfectly normally. And, even if I was to be over-enthusiastic

with my toothbrush, what does it matter? What harm is it doing to anyone? Who is going to judge me? Nobody.

So, I try to not take the voices' words too seriously. Often, after having forgotten their remarks, I will stumble upon my earlier notes and laugh at the power they once had over me.

Noting down what your voices say can create a refreshing distance between you and them. This method is especially helpful to provide a reality check when your voices make you doubt yourself.

3. **Listen to music.** I know that, for some people, this can help to drown out voices. Unfortunately, it doesn't work for me – my voices just shout louder over the music! – but maybe you could benefit from it? Whether you listen to heavy metal, classical music or pop is up to you.

4. **Keep yourself occupied.** In the early stages of recovery, you might not feel ready to be busy in a "normal" context – school, job, hobbies, sports, etc. If this is the case, scroll aimlessly through social media all you want and take the time out you need to recover. Origami, gentle exercising, watching music videos, reading, solving Sudoku or crosswords, taking a free online personality test and doing a puzzle are all things that I tried, but you should find something that appeals to you. If you find yourself able to cope with it, you might try writing down small goals that you would like to achieve so that you have something to work toward. You could go for a walk with a friend or family member, as long as you're not overwhelmed by the impressions that being outdoors can create – too much input can trigger voices. Take things in incremental stages at a pace that works for you, and try your best not to come to a complete standstill. At this point, I think it is important for me to acknowledge that I fully understand that everyone's lives are different: I do not have the responsibility of raising children, nor the pressure to be the main breadwinner in the family – so my perspective on the early days of recovery is one that is personal to my situation, and I can only offer advice on things that helped me.

Keep in mind that your voices may go away while you're distracted, but they might come back with a vengeance later when your guard is down. Understandably, this can be extremely distressing. You may think, "What have I done? Why won't they go away? Why are they worse? How can I ever do that activity again if the voices are just going to attack me afterwards?" I know I did, and it discouraged me from trying for a long time. However, I've found that by being prepared for this to happen and planning your downtime accordingly is a help – make sure you factor in plenty of rest time after any activity. My rule of thumb is not to make more than one social arrangement a week, as I need so much time to recuperate afterwards.

5. **Talk back.** If you are on your own, tell those voices – out loud – to "shut the hell up!"

CHAPTER 29
WHAT THE VOICES SAY

When my voices were at their worst, I had over 200 of them – yes, you read that correctly.

I couldn't concentrate, speak or think straight. It was impossible to distance myself from so much noise, and that's why antipsychotic medication was a godsend. Once the medicine started to take effect, it removed most of my voices and allowed me the breathing space I desperately needed to focus on my recovery without all the chaos in my head. It transformed my life.

Voices are sneaky and crop up when you least expect them, making them unpredictable and very tough to cope with. At their most pervasive, I found it useful to write down what they said, as soon as they said it. This requires concentration and that you have a phone or notebook on you at all times. Frustratingly, if I didn't register the comments immediately, I would forget them – another interesting aspect of hearing voices on which I will now elaborate.

Schizophrenia can be a living nightmare. Voices are like bad dreams – the kind that make perfect sense at the time but are immediately forgotten as soon as you regain "consciousness". Interestingly, when I managed to write down what they were saying, I would read the words and think, "Well, this is just nonsense!" It gave me a completely different perspective on them: in my head, they had power over me; on paper, they looked ridiculous.

Funny, isn't it?

Here are some things they'd say, divided into positive, neutral and negative:

Positive: "She's doing well. She looks great. She's awesome. She can conquer the world. She's a creative genius. He likes her. They think she's cute. What a lovely girl."

Neutral: "She's wearing a red T-shirt today. She's brushing her teeth. She has schizophrenia. She's an ambitious one."

Negative: "Shut up. We hate you. We think you're weird. Sophie is going to dump you as a friend. What's she doing here? She's doing a rubbish job. Don't say that – they'll laugh at you. Don't eat that, you'll get sick. Don't wear that, you'll look stupid. You're worthless. Look at yourself... loser."

When they said nice things – mostly during my childhood – I would believe them. When they said negative things, which happened during my breakdown, I believed them.

Today, my voices are mainly neutral, which is, in part, due to the medication that I take, but also because I've found a groove that works for me. The life I have created suits my specific requirements and, although somewhat limited compared to what others might consider a normal existence, it works for me. In my case, it must be like this, otherwise I risk relapse and falling ill again. It has taken many years, but I now recognize and understand what can threaten my mental health, and I am happy to structure a life around that framework. I still cannot do very much outside of my regular routines – ceramics once a week, occasional visits with my friends, writing my blog – and I require a lot of downtime. But as long as I don't expose myself to undue stress, either positive or negative, I won't trigger my voices. And thank goodness for that!

CHAPTER 30
THE BREAKDOWN

Okay, I've been delaying writing this chapter.

It's taken me years – a decade – to accept the idea of explaining what a full-blown psychotic breakdown feels like. I must tread carefully because it can be painful to relive that time. As mentioned previously, it was an extremely stressful time for me and everyone around me. But this is a book about schizophrenia, and I don't think it would be complete without a chapter describing the experience of a full psychotic breakdown.

Psychosis is often first noticed from an outside perspective – how *other* people see and experience it. That was how I initially began to understand that something was wrong with me. My family and friends were the first to comment on the changes in my behaviour and point out that I didn't appear to be myself. I certainly wasn't well enough to acknowledge it at the time, as I was deep into my psychosis at that point. In fact, I became furious if my family suggested that I was behaving strangely.

So, what does it feel like to be the one *experiencing* psychosis?

Well, to be honest, I didn't feel any difference at all. The keyword here is *feel*. As far as I was concerned, I felt fine, wasn't aware of any shift in my emotional state and didn't think my behaviour was strange. In retrospect, I *was* thinking differently but, at the time, I didn't think that I was thinking differently – if you see what I mean!

My mum often asks if I can remember anything from my breakdown. To be honest, when I was first discharged from hospital, it was *waaaaaay* too raw for me to even begin to explain what I was experiencing; too new, too painful, too embarrassing. I felt very ashamed about the things I'd done – even though I now understand, as do my family, that I had no control over my actions at the time. However, it's incredibly difficult to distinguish between healthy and ill behaviours when, as far as you're concerned, you were feeling fine!

The binbags

At one point during my psychosis, I felt the urge to get rid of everything I had. I filled some bin bags with stuff from my room and… just let them sit there. My mum asked me many times if she could remove them and take them to the recycling centre, but I wouldn't allow her to do it. Eventually, because they had old food in them, the bin bags attracted tons of fruit flies, and Mum made an executive decision to throw them out. I need to explain that, at the time, I was incredibly sensitive about anyone being in my room, and my family were doing their best to respect that, no matter how bizarre my behaviour. However, in this case, the unpleasant scent from the binbags and the fruit fly convention they were hosting forced my mum's hand. On this occasion, I didn't protest – I was too far gone to have any real comprehension of what was happening, and my mum had to decide between a smelly house full of flies or triggering me. I am sure that there were things in those bin bags that should not have been thrown out by me, but how was my mum supposed to know that? I seem to remember that I put my school art folder in one of the bags. This saddens me because that folder represented a big part of my time at gymnasium. I can't remember much else of what went out, but I still have painful moments where I suddenly think, "Aaargh, did I throw *that* out too?!" and need to find a way to calm myself or search for the item in question. This might not seem like a big deal to some people, but if one places sentimental value on objects and hates to throw things away, it can be distressing and a genuine jolt to the system.

Yellow papers

The episode where I went to the police station. I had just been sectioned on yellow papers by my doctor. Yellow papers are typically prepared by the patient's general practitioner. A patient can be forcibly admitted to a psychiatric ward if the following two conditions are met:

1. The patient is psychotic – meaning they have lost contact with reality – or is in a state equatable with this. Otherwise, it would be unjustifiable not to detain the person in question for treatment because the prospect of a cure, or a significant and decisive improvement in the condition, will otherwise be significantly impaired.
2. The person in question presents an imminent and significant danger to himself or others. In the second case, red papers are issued.

The doctor's statement must be based on the doctor's own examination of the patient. Before the decision on the use of coercion is made, the patient must be thoroughly informed about the intended use of coercion, as well as the background for this and its purpose. He or she must be allowed to think about it. However, in some cases, the situation can be so acute and aggravated that this period of reflection must be short. According to the law, the information must be both oral and written, but in practice it can be difficult to inform in writing. Compulsory hospitalization must not take place in a ward where the doctor or GP himself is employed.

In actuality, the first step is to try to persuade the patient to go voluntarily. If this is impossible, the patient is informed that the doctor will issue yellow papers for the purpose of involuntary hospitalization. The medical certificate is sent or handed over to the police for approval by the Chief of Police, who will forward the statement to a psychiatric ward with a request that the patient be received. The chief physician of the psychiatric ward in question must approve the involuntary admission documents before the patient can be admitted. In the absence of the chief physician, the decision may be made by another physician in the psychiatric ward. It is then the task of the police to pick up the patient and transport them to the receiving ward. In some cases, yellow papers can be enacted immediately with an agreement from the receiving department. This may be the case, for example, when the patient is already in a psychiatric emergency room or in a general practitioner's surgery. As much as is possible, the inpatient doctor must be present when the patient is picked up by the police, who make sure to inform the doctor of the time they implemented the involuntary hospitalization. It is my understanding that police are involved in this process to protect vulnerable people by ensuring there is no fraudulent sectioning of an individual just because they are a nuisance, rather than being in true need of psychiatric care. Once yellow papers are issued, the matter is out of the hands of the patient and the police are required to escort them to the hospital within a week.

As is required by law, I had been given a copy of the papers and, seeing the word *politi* (police in Danish), I decided to take matters into my own hands. I cycled directly to the police station and asked them to revoke it! I needed to inform them that I was perfectly fine, and they should cancel the yellow papers immediately. I didn't tell my parents where I was going – in fact, they had no idea that I was there until the police phoned them. On arrival, I approached a policeman behind the reception desk, showed him the yellow papers, said, "Hello, please could you…" and promptly burst into tears! After months of chaos and distress, the floodgates opened and I was a sobbing, incoherent wreck.

A very kind and sympathetic policeman sat me down, offered me some tissues and a cup of hot chocolate, and gently enquired if we should contact my parents. At this point in my breakdown, I was so distressed, confused and disorientated that my anger – rage! – was focused toward my parents. They were the *last* people I wanted to call. They were the *last* people I wanted to see. *They* were the enemy! However, after some persuasion, I finally conceded, and the police called them. Within minutes, my exhausted, confused and somewhat shocked parents arrived and clarified the situation. I couldn't make eye contact with them and would only communicate via the policeman. I told him, shouting for emphasis, "I will go to the hospital, but only if THEY DON'T COME!" To that, the policeman replied, "Would you go, if I got two of my nice friends to take you?" I agreed. That is a vision that has stayed with my parents ever since: their 17-year-old daughter, in the back of a police car, being driven to a psychiatric hospital. Without them.

(Note: I have been helped with some of the above recollections by my mum, as I was so unwell at the time of being sectioned that some of the details are a bit fuzzy in my memory.)

Some impressions from the hospital: my first few nights were spent in the closed unit with only a couple of other patients. One of the patients was extremely quiet, only speaking in a whisper at dinner time to criticize the food. The other patient, a friendly girl, regularly tried to strike up conversation and gave me little lip balms as gifts. Then, one night, she suddenly started hitting herself on the head and screaming. She had told me in an earlier conversation that she heard voices – and then I got to witness how it affected her.

During this time, I was also introduced to patients in the open unit – before the nurses decided it was best for me to stay in the closed unit to prevent me from becoming overwhelmed. I remember sitting next to a girl in the open unit who asked if I wanted to play cards with her. I shook my head; "No." I think I was so bewildered by everything going on that I was unable to engage in any kind of normal social behaviour. Contact, of any kind, was confusing and exhausting, and even the simple act of playing cards was too much for my shattered brain.

Communication was impossible in the early days: I remember having a splitting headache but being unable to tell the nurses and, on another occasion, sitting on the floor with my head buried in my knees as I rocked back and forth, incapable of expressing what I needed or felt. I have memories of staring at a radiator and one of the nurses repeatedly asking me, "Can you see something that we can't?" I also remember taking the mattress from my bed, putting it on the floor in a corner of my hospital room and sleeping there, rather than using the bed. I was later informed that this was commonly seen in psychotic patients whose whole reality was askew. Sometimes the floor was the only thing that appeared to be stable, so it made sense that they should feel safer lying on it rather than anywhere else in their room.

Before I was admitted to hospital, I'd missed appointments with my psychiatrist because I just hadn't shown up. Now, due to the enforced monotony of life in the closed unit, seeing my psychiatrist felt like a luxury and a welcome break in a long string of dull days. When I was first admitted to the hospital, my parents were advised not to visit me for the first couple of weeks – partly because I was so psychotic that it would be of no help to me or them, and partly because I required complete isolation in order to try to stabilize me. Once that time had passed, they visited daily – sometimes twice a day. Conversation wasn't really possible, so, to fill the time, we went for very short walks around the hospital grounds. This helped to ease the boredom of being incarcerated and gently reintroduced me to my parents and some semblance of normality.

It's strange how the mind works – I was completely incapable of functioning normally, but still believed that my feelings and responses to life around me *were* normal. Until my breakdown, my definition of being ill had been, "Unless I'm throwing up or bleeding from a main artery, I'm fine." I hadn't ever considered the psychological aspect of illness, so how was I to know what it felt like? What could I compare my current experience with? I think the reason many psychotic patients don't understand that we are ill is because we *cannot* understand that we are ill, if you see what I mean. We may have a vague sense that something's wrong but, if we've never been educated about psychosis or don't know anybody who suffers from mental health issues, most of us will have no clue about it. I didn't know that hearing voices wasn't a normal experience – I had heard them all my life and just assumed that everyone else did too – and believed that the gradual failing of my cognitive symptoms was just me being stupid.

Schizophrenia is a brain disease. Your brain is control central, and everything you experience originates from and is processed by it. So, what happens when your brain suddenly starts sending faulty messages? It's your brain, you've trusted it all your life – so, of course you're going to believe what it tells you.

Naturally, it was my family and friends who first noticed something was wrong – they could see that my behaviour was hugely out of character, as were my mannerisms, my speech and my attitude. I just wasn't myself, but it was impossible to get through to me when I was so unwell because I simply didn't believe them, and the paranoid aspect of my illness meant I also didn't trust them. To be honest, I'm not sure how one does get through to someone experiencing psychosis – how do you convince them that *their* reality is not real?

This can be an extremely frustrating and deeply painful experience for everyone involved. The sufferer thinks that their family and friends are plotting against them, and the concerned parties are at their wits' end trying to persuade their loved one that they are severely ill. This can go on for months – years! – and, in some cases, the situation never gets resolved, particularly if the sufferer is over the age of 18 and legally considered able to make their own decisions, no matter how severely ill they may be.

CHAPTER 31
ONLINE

The future is digital. Rapid advancements in technology have revolutionized our world, and most of us use social media to connect and communicate, perhaps even more comfortably than in real life (IRL). We're always on, we're always connected.

I've always escaped into the internet. When I was younger, I would play Neopets for hours, then I graduated to Google to search for song lyrics and pictures of characters from my favourite manga. Upon discharge from hospital, I read every internet resource I could find about schizophrenia. In my hope of connecting with people, I read masses of articles on how to succeed socially and created profiles on dating and social networking sites – but ended up deleting them all when I realized I wasn't invested enough to use them. Today, I rely on Google to check my grammar and pronunciation and as a dictionary and thesaurus. I read how-to guides online for just about everything from how to fold a jumper to how to flirt! I use YouTube to watch all my favourite music videos and post regularly to Facebook and Instagram, where I've established artist and author platforms. I have a Twitter profile and connect with other writers under the hashtag #WritingCommunity, and I also use Blogger and my website to post my articles about living with schizophrenia.

Cyberbullying is rampant on the internet. I have experienced it and, although it wasn't excessive, it was enough for me to understand that it is a real and widespread problem. However, there are many good aspects to social media, and search engines have changed my life for the better. Everything you need to know is available on Google and other search platforms. Why pay for classes when you can find almost anything you want to learn online and, in many cases, free of charge? Without social media, I wouldn't have been able to share my blog to a wider audience or re-connect with old friends. I find it much easier to communicate with people online, with the protection of my keyboard, where I have the time to formulate what I would like to say, instead of feeling awkward and on the spot as I often do in real-life social situations. Life would have been so boring – and rather lonely – without access to the internet and the good possibilities it has offered someone like me. I don't want to think about how much worse off I'd have been, had I believed that there was nothing more for me than the unpleasant bubble in which I found myself.

When you have schizophrenia, it is quite likely that you may isolate yourself more than other people due to the nature of your illness. This can lead to a *lot* of screen time. If used carefully, the internet can be a safe harbour for people who might feel overwhelmed by the many stresses involved in daily connection in the real world. That's not to say that one should live by the internet alone – not at all. It is just a very useful tool for those of us who would like to communicate, learn and connect with the world – just in a way that works for us.

CHAPTER 32
READING

I didn't pick up a book for many years after my breakdown.

Having been an avid reader as a child, this was distressing for me. How could I not read? I loved reading! It had always been one of my all-time favourite things to do. Getting lost in the world of fiction was something I really missed in the early stages of my recovery. The truth was, I just couldn't face it. The simple act of picking up a book and starting to read was overwhelming – an insurmountable task. Furthermore, I was afraid I would put myself off reading completely if I tried too hard. Although it was very frustrating at the time, in retrospect, I understand it. At the beginning of my recovery, even five minutes of TV would exhaust me, so reading a book was pretty much out of the question. I hadn't come far enough in my recovery for my brain to keep focus for any length of time. However, I was determined I would manage it again.

I began small. Initially, I read books about schizophrenia because learning about something relatable was helpful. I also read books about how to gain confidence, overcome social anxiety and be the best version of myself, as well as a couple of easily digestible psychology and philosophy titles. I was interested in understanding myself and others, so this seemed like a logical way to do it. Then, I ordered copies of my favourite manga books that I had missed since my breakdown. I love manga and the addition of dynamic, appealing drawings made for a more manageable reading experience.

The first novel I managed to read post-breakdown was *Skallagrigg* by William Horwood. My mum had suggested it to me, and I loved it. It is a poignant, uplifting story and exactly what I needed to read at that time. I am not sure that it is still available in bookshops but, if you can find a copy, I highly recommend it.

I soon got hooked on reading again, devouring the first three instalments of the *Harry Potter* series, which I'd enjoyed as a child, and I started feeling my creative inspiration returning in waves. Next: Marie Kondo's *The Life-Changing Magic of Tidying*, which I downloaded on my phone and promptly finished.

Now, I'm a member of a book-streaming service and listen to audiobooks, which is a great way of reading if you don't have the time or energy to sit down with a physical book – or if you like to multi-task and listen to a book while you're doing the hoovering!

It is not uncommon for people struck by psychosis to find themselves suddenly incapable of managing things they had previously enjoyed. This is my experience, and I'm still nowhere near as avid a reader as I was when I was younger. However, I'm not beating myself up about it anymore or comparing myself to anyone else. When one has schizophrenia, everything is overwhelming – just making a choice in a bookshop can be daunting. Where do I start? Which book is right? What do I want to read? What if there are many things that I want to read but can't choose? I try not to discourage myself. Should I choose a book that is familiar to me or try one that I haven't heard of, but looks interesting? I have an excellent public library very close to my home, but that would involve being in an unfamiliar environment with lots of strangers, and I am not convinced I would remember to return the books on time.

All that ambivalence…

I have a profile on Goodreads, which combines reading books, giving reviews and seeing what my friends are reading. Being a social person – ironically enough! – this is quite an inspiring experience for me. I only review books if I've enjoyed them and always award five stars: if I didn't like a book, why waste time spreading negativity about it? I'd much rather share my enjoyment of a favourite read. At least I'm not ambivalent about that. #KeepItPositive

Speaking of ambivalence, this brings me to my next set of coping strategies.

COPING STRATEGIES – AMBIVALENCE

So, how does one cope with ambivalence?
I have a few tips:

1. If you're ambivalent about which socks to wear for the day, hold one in each hand and try to visualize which one you'd rather wear. If you don't know, make a snap decision on one of them and then pay attention to how that makes you feel. Does it feel like the wrong decision? If so, go with the other ones. Conversely, if your first choice felt right, stick with that. I realize that this reads like a great big bowl of indecision, but that's what much of my life – and ambivalence – is about. *Sigh.*

2. Remind yourself that the choices you make can always have negative or positive consequences. Any decision has the potential to be a wrong one, but even if that's the case, it could eventually lead to something good. You may make a decision that you regret in the short term but find it benefits you in the long term. We're all human, we're all learning, and nobody gets it right every time. For me, the best thing to do is not to get bogged down with regret and anxiety regarding the choices I make, but keep moving forward and doing my best. I always try to keep in mind that, by not letting myself be pressured into making decisions in a rush, I'll probably do just fine.

3. Listen to your ambivalence. It's telling you something. Do you *really* want to go to that party? Are you *genuinely* interested in signing up for that course? Would you actually prefer to eat the pasta, rather than the fish that the waiter is recommending? We are faced with so many offers, pressures and temptations every day, it's impossible to make the best decision all the time. Sometimes,

I find that I try to live up to what I think *others* expect of me or to adjust to certain societal norms while completely ignoring my own gut feeling or logical reasoning. It has taken time, but I have learned that sometimes it is better to press the pause button on a decision and listen to what my ambivalence is *really* saying to me before I decide. Obviously, this tactic doesn't work so well in a restaurant – one must be considerate of the working hours of the waiter!

4. Sometimes, you must take action on the spot – ambivalence or not – and try not to delay the people waiting behind you in the queue at the baker's while you ruminate over all the delicious cakes on offer. Luckily, my local bakery has an app with the option to click and collect: I can take all the time I need to browse their assortment from home and pay directly via the app. Then, I just pop into the bakery, pick up my ready-for-collection order and leave – no muss, no fuss. If this would be a help to you, see if any of your favourite shops have this option. The modern world is increasingly online and, although it can mean we lose out on social interaction, it is really great for people like me with schizophrenia. Long live the cake app!

5. If you're ever in a situation where you must make a swift decision and you feel uncomfortable with the outcome, talk to someone you trust about it. Don't stress over it on your own.

6. Make a pros and cons list. I use this option for bigger decisions that don't have to be made straight away.

7. Finally, I try to keep in mind that, no matter what decision I make, no matter what message I choose to send or whichever dish I opt for at the restaurant, I can always justify my choice to myself. This has been a revelation: realizing that I will be fine with my choices – as long as they're not dangerous or illegal! – so why stress over them beforehand? It may take a while to realize the positives of a decision, but they're always there.

8. Oh, and one more tip: if it helps you, try not to view each choice as a drastic point of no return. Often things hold greater gravity in our own heads than in real life. In fact, the more decisions you make, the better you'll get at making them – at least, that's what I believe (as I pop the 15th chocolate caramel into my mouth...).

CHAPTER 33
MESSY ROOM, MESSY MIND?

I've heard it expressed that "a messy room equals a messy head". However, there is also an opposing school of thought which suggests "messy room, creative mind"! My mum diplomatically refers to my mess as an artistic environment, which, coming from a staunch minimalist, should be taken as a compliment...

A task that I often have difficulty with is keeping things in order and tidying up. In the early days after my release from hospital, I couldn't tidy my room at all – my head just wasn't in the right zone, and it seemed too big a hurdle to get over. On the rare occasion that I felt able to try, I might manage ten minutes of clearing up and then zone out in the middle of my room, my motivation fading, and I'd be unable to continue. The task seemed insurmountable. It is important to stress that I didn't lose interest in what I was doing – I just lost the ability to see my way forward through the mess. For months, over half of my bed was covered with notebooks, pens, books, receipts, handbags and the clothes I couldn't face hanging up. All my drawers and any available storage boxes were stuffed full of things I hadn't looked at for many years.

I hated it.

I absolutely loathed the state my bedroom was in and was far too embarrassed to invite friends over. It wasn't the way I wanted my room to look – it wasn't the way I wanted me to look – but I couldn't bring myself to throw anything out. Ambivalence kicked in, and I suddenly had to keep the old, faded top I couldn't fit into anymore, the crumpled plastic bag that might come in useful, the odd bits of paper and string that peppered the floor. I couldn't let them go, but neither could I explain why. It was awful. I was unable to part with *anything* – paperclips, half-torn labels, old shopping receipts – because I was genuinely scared that I might need them later and feared the repercussions of getting rid of them. It was a combination of fear and ambivalence that controlled my actions… and kept me stuck in a cluttered mess. It was a few years before I finally felt able to up my game and do something about it.

IMPORTANT ADVICE: family, friends or carers should *not* take over and tidy up for their loved one. It will not be viewed as a helpful deed – if anything, it will prove counter-productive – and will cause indescribable stress for the person you are trying to help. An uninvited surprise clear-out would have left me devastated and set my progress back severely. My room is my space, and it's up to me to deal with it and live with it. This didn't mean I couldn't be gently nudged in the right direction, but it needed to be done with patience and empathy in order to have the correct outcome. My parents would often comment on the mess and suggest I try to tidy up "just a little bit", but they also understood enough to give me plenty of space to reach that conclusion myself. Once I began to recover, I was more able to make decisions myself and gradually began the slow process of clearing up.

I approached it systematically – one drawer at a time. It felt good to see the drawer gradually become emptier, but progress was painfully slow and required many rest stops. Over time, I was able to work my way through most of the room and, if I took it in bite-size pieces, as Mum always recommends, I was able to cope with the emotions and stress of working through the guddle. In a way, my bedroom was like a metaphor for my brain – chaotic and much in need of re-structuring! In the beginning, I needed a lot of validation from my parents to assure me that I was doing a good job and that I would not regret any throwing-away decisions. It is important to remember this when you are dealing with anyone struggling with mental illness: small steps, empathy and understanding are essential factors in helping them to move forward.

Nowadays, I am far more able to keep my living space relatively organized in my own way. However, a consequence of the new Georgia is that I sometimes end up unable to find anything... because it's been moved from its usual place!

I hope this chapter provides a little insight into the conflict some of us experience when trying to create order out of our chaos – and perhaps it might kick-start you too.

CHAPTER 34
ADULT LIFE / INDEPENDENCE

The transition to adult life can be difficult for any young person and, when you have schizophrenia, those challenges are multiplied.

I used to feel like I was very far behind my friends in terms of maturity and grown-up milestones. At the time of writing, I'm 27, living at home, have never had a boyfriend, can't drive, couldn't finish my education and can't hold down a job. You get the picture. But all is not lost! I have managed to build a life that works for me and one in which I'm happy.

My life was radically changed when I had my psychosis and, despite my very best efforts, some things are no longer an option for me. In recovery, good health takes priority – it took some time for me to understand this – and requires that other things are put on hold or cancelled altogether. For a while, I tried very hard to finish my education and hold down a job but, ultimately, I was unable to cope with what those responsibilities required. Over time, I have had to accept my "behind-ness", but it's been a long process getting there. The first step was making peace with the fact that I couldn't attend school or cope with full-time employment, no matter how much I wanted it nor how hard I tried. Instead, I would need to create a completely new path – tailored to fit my abilities. In the past, I thought I had to have a boyfriend, had to complete a formal education, had to follow the path of school to job to husband to children when, in fact, none of it was right for me. I didn't thrive in the Danish education system, and a regular job had proved too much for me. As for finding a man to spend the rest of my life with, well, lovely as that might be, I know now it is not something I had or have to achieve to be happy.

I'm not suggesting that *you* should drop out of your education, nor give up on attempts to find a job or a good relationship. There are many people living with schizophrenia who have managed to carve out completely different lives from mine and are successful partners, parents, employees or employers, and have been able to complete an advanced education. I am just saying that, unfortunately, that has not been my experience. Obviously, I can only discuss things from my viewpoint and explain how I have found my place in this world. The life I have built is one that works for me.

One of the reasons I can now live a relatively independent life is thanks to the Danish benefits system and the financial support it provides. Danes are subject to the highest taxation in the world, which helps to create a safety net for those of us who have fallen off the high wire. But they don't just dole it out to anyone...

I thought only OAPs received a pension.

During my time in the psychiatric support system, attending courses and groups created for people coping with their first psychosis, I was given a variety of options to further my education and/or enter the workplace. I tried everything that was offered to me – and more! – but it eventually became clear that I was not equipped to handle it. After several years of assessment, interspersed with interviews by medical professionals and social workers, I was asked to complete a series of questionnaires in which my parents, medical team and the people who had been involved in my education or employment had to give their honest appraisals of me. This proved to be a particularly brutal task for the wonderful friends who had tried to help me by offering me the chance to work at their publishing house and ceramics studio. They really did not want to write anything negative about my efforts because they cared about me and felt it would be neither kind nor helpful. However, they were informed that no matter how fond of me they were, it was their honest opinion of my abilities that was required to provide an accurate assessment. They were going to have to be cruel to be kind. Their sensitive-but-honest evaluations were additional evidence that my shattered brain was simply unable to cope with the myriad of things that normal brains take for granted in the educational and employment arena. It all sounds rather harsh, but it was a necessary process to establish what I was capable of and whether I could function in a regular work or educational environment. After the final interview (one of several with social workers, my psychiatrist and doctor, representatives from the town council, my parents and I), it was agreed that I was eligible for a disability pension, *førtidspension* in Danish. Being awarded a disability pension before the age of 40 is relatively unusual in Denmark. Ironically, it is the larger, wealthier municipalities, like the one we live in, that can be reticent about it because, with a big population to look after, their budgets are often stretched to the limit. The fact that I was considered eligible by our municipality was a great relief to me and my parents, who both burst into tears at the meeting when it was confirmed I would receive a pension.

Everyone I met in the psychiatric support system had been unfailingly kind and helpful, but it was a great relief that the years of being assessed were now at an end. Sometimes, it felt like I was being pushed beyond my limits by well-intentioned people who didn't comprehend the realities of living with paranoid schizophrenia. That, together with my genuine wish to be a good patient and do everything expected of me, was a draining combination that would often result in an increase in voices, communication problems, exhaustion and an inability to motivate myself. After years of trying – and my parents fighting for me every step of the way – I finally felt validated. And secure.

Being on disability pension means that there is no further expectation for me to enter education or the workforce unless I choose to do so. If I am being honest, though, I think the method of assessing individuals is not necessarily fair. It is a very protracted affair and doesn't take into consideration the impact that schizophrenia or any type of psychosis has on an individual, particularly in relation to cognitive, communication and social skills. How can one be assertive or express one's needs in the workplace when the simple act of talking is exhausting? How does one cope with social interaction, group work, forward-planning and communication in the classroom when cognitive skills are damaged and audible or visual hallucinations are present? Public transport can be a nightmare too: people, physical contact, remembering to punch your ticket, route planning, possible cancellations, smells, lights, noise – and that's before you've even arrived at your destination. Add to that the possibility that your medicine's side effects can kick in at any time – in public – and you have a stress-overload recipe for disaster. In my experience, the unquestioned assumption of a return to education and employment is often unrealistic and does not appear to embrace the very specific problems faced by those of us who suffer from paranoid schizophrenia.

Had I not had the support of my parents, I know that I would not have been able to cope. They went to every meeting, asked the important questions, drove me to and from the courses and appointments I had to attend, acted as my voice when I simply couldn't communicate, helped me to complete any paperwork required – patiently explaining it to me every step of the way – and let me know that their home was always my home, thus relieving the municipality of the cost and responsibility of providing housing for me. They managed to navigate a way through the bureaucracy on my behalf, always courteous to everyone they dealt with, but absolutely determined to get me the help I required. If it wasn't for them, I think I'd still be floating around in the system today.

I can only imagine how confusing and frightening it must be for anyone who does not have that kind of support – the ones who fall through the safety net. It should be a priority politically, financially and socially that support for those with mental health issues is continually assessed and improved to ensure they get the *right* kind of help.

UPDATE: while there are still many things I cannot do – for the moment, anyway – I will soon be taking a giant leap forward into independence. By the time this book is published, I'll have moved into my first flat and started to live a little more independently. So, I can put a great big tick on my "How to be an Adult" checklist – woohoo!

CHAPTER 35
"WEIRD"

Who decides what's weird?

I've been thinking about this lately... the concept of weird.

I've never seen myself as weird, and I don't find a lot of other people weird. We're all human. Anything a human can experience has been experienced by humans before and will be experienced by humans in the future – no matter how strange or embarrassing it feels at the time.

I have had a lot of feedback from people saying they thought they were "just a weirdo" until they read my blog and realized someone else was going through the same things. It's wonderful that they've found comfort in my blog, but also a bit sad that they've felt like a freak up until then. As I said before, I started my blog partly to create what I felt was missing in my world – in other words, what I'd have found beneficial to read – and also to express myself. It was a space for me to vent my thoughts, feelings and experiences in the manner that is most comfortable for me: writing. I needed to communicate and connect, reach out and show others who I am. I felt stifled by years of bullying and exclusion and felt compelled to put into words the reason why I had dropped out of school. I wanted to write the truth about me and what I had been through. I wasn't comfortable with disclosing my diagnosis initially, which is why, in the early years, we kept it private, with only my family and close friends being aware of the real situation.

However, as soon as I "came clean" and began telling people I had schizophrenia, I found it to be a relief. People responded *so* kindly and were very accepting of my illness. I guess I'd been worried they'd distance themselves from me or not know how to deal with it, but, if anything, I've become even closer to my friends since I told them! Of course, nobody should be rejected for their diagnosis, but stigma is real when it comes to mental health and especially schizophrenia.

So, to get back to the point: weirdness. What do you consider weird? What would you find strange in another person? What aspects of yourself are you reticent about sharing with others out of fear they'll shun you? What is something you enjoy or like that others might find weird?

My family have a nickname for me: "limited edition". They say, "She's not weird, she's limited edition!" I like that. They even bought me a cap with "Limited Edition" printed on it. In our family we can see the lighter side of life, and when you are dealing with severe mental illness, a sense of humour is essential. Plus, having humour about my quirks – and putting an affectionate label on them – has made it easier for us all to deal with it. "Limited edition" works for me because it acknowledges my sometimes unconventional behaviour without being cruel about it. I think it's important to maintain a sense of humour and not be shy about making light-hearted observations about the situation if the moment merits it. It's true that "laughter is the best medicine," though please don't give up your antipsychotics! Having said that, my family are also very aware of the fine line between treating my situation with humour and knowing when the situation calls for another kind of approach entirely – empathy, patience, dialogue, boundaries – and medicine!

So, the next time someone calls you "weirdo", just tell them, "I am not weird – I am limited edition!"

I think I may have come across as weird to my contemporaries – or, at least, that's how I've felt. People don't shun someone unless they find them too difficult to understand, and I have never been an unkind person or someone who deserved to be ignored, so perhaps they found me strange? Again, I've never personally identified as weird, but I can't see myself from the outside, so all my thoughts and behaviour make perfect sense to me. Yes, I cringe when I remember some of my past actions – don't we all? – but I don't believe I've done anything inherently *wrong*. Maybe that's where the line goes. The line between *my* perception and other people's perception. In my eyes, if you're not mistreating anyone, it doesn't matter if you drone on about something dull, dance by yourself at parties or need to ascertain the difference between Indian and African elephants (it's the ears). It doesn't bother me, and I don't think you're weird. We all make fools of ourselves sometimes and can all be a bit "limited edition" in our own way – so why not just accept people for who they are, quirks and all? Call me naïve, but I think weirdness is a spectrum on which everyone falls somewhere. Everybody's a bit weird if you scratch the surface. What is considered weird to one, might be normal to another.

However, there is nothing a bully likes more than someone who doesn't fit into the pack. Being bullied and excluded gives you a lot of time to sit alone and speculate about what you're doing wrong. So, I have had plenty of opportunity to wonder what it could have been that caused my peers to exclude me. I scrutinized every aspect of myself in the search for why I was failing. Nothing I did seemed to help. It appeared that I was just not acceptable to them. As I write this, I'm listening to one of my favourite songs, "Nobody's Fool" by Avril Lavigne. I hope you'll look up the first verse of the track because she really hits the nail on the head!

Although I withdrew into myself while trying to figure it all out, I never went against my personal integrity; I did my best to stay true to myself and not lose my spark, even through all the chaos. My dad would often say to me, "Just be yourself, Georgia – stay true to who you are – that is all you can do. And, if they don't like it, that's their loss!" Maybe my refusal to bow to peer pressure – and keeping my core personality intact – is what earned me the label of weird, but things would have got too messy inside my head if I had lost myself in order to fit in.

Perhaps weird is a good trait. Some of the most innovative, creative and wealthiest people in the world could be considered weird by normal parameters. I'd rather be weird and comfortable in my own skin than try to fit in and suffer. I might seem weird (Mum: "You're not!") but I have helped many people with my blog and my writing. I might seem weird, but I know what I want from life. I might seem weird, but I'm kind, sensitive, creative and determined. I might seem weird to you, but I'm not weird to me and, frankly, I'm okay with that.

(Note: there's a difference between weird and being downright dodgy – and hopefully most people can distinguish between the two. #DodgyIsNotGood)

CHAPTER 36
SLEEP AND REST

No downtime, no up time.

We all benefit from periods of rest where nothing is expected of us, so we can kick back and relax. These breaks from our usual routine can take many forms – what suits a CEO might not do it for a ballet dancer – so it is important to find the chill zone that works for you.

For anyone who lives with mental illness, my advice would be to view rest periods as a necessary and beneficial component of your recovery. It's taken me a long time to get used to the fact that I cannot be as consistently active and engaged as I would like to. To remain healthy, I must decompress and recharge regularly. However, instead of thinking, "Ugh, this is so stupid, why do I have to slow down? I should be doing things!" I remind myself that recovery is like a muscle, which means it requires both activity *and* rest to stay strong. You shouldn't strain your muscles, so why strain your brain?

In the past, I hated to rest when I felt I should be doing more. My mind would fight the enforced inactivity every step of the way: pulse racing, body tense; I usually ended up feeling worse. I require a *lot* of stimulation and activity to keep me ticking over, but I'm learning to make time for sleep if I need it, even during the day. Sleep doesn't solve all my problems, but it helps me refocus and gain perspective, and I often feel a sense of calm and clarity on waking. In the past, taking a nap felt like giving up – but now I realize that, for me, it is an integral part of my recovery.

COPING STRATEGIES –
ART, MUSIC AND WRITING

ART AND CERAMICS:

I love being creative, but it can trigger feelings of pressure and perfectionism in me. I often have to fight *my own* expectations of my talent – no room for error! I occasionally accept private commissions which, although flattering and encouraging, can be a recipe for stress because I worry that I will not be able to live up to my clients' expectations. As soon as creating starts to feel like expectation, it freaks me out, and I find myself unable to produce anything. I am also terrible at handling even the slightest hint of criticism, but I am working on that and getting much better at seeing it for what it is – a constructive tool to improve my skills. Having said that, I have never had anyone who was unhappy with the work I did for them – whew!

Drawing, painting and working with ceramics are things I do for fun and enjoyment and are not things I use as a coping mechanism. When I'm feeling fragile, to embark on a painting or a ceramics project would be counterproductive. Instead, when I feel under pressure, I always turn to writing – something I have done since I was a very young child. I have always had a love of notebooks and, over the years, I have written hundreds of thousands of words within their pages. I simply cannot imagine how I would manage if I could not write. It is a lifesaver for me.

MUSIC:

When I am trying to work through something, one of my best home remedies is listening to a specific song on repeat. How does this work for me?

Step 1: Choose a song I love (and can listen to several times on repeat).

Step 2: Make myself comfortable and ensure I won't be disturbed for a while – phone notifications off!

Step 3: Focus on the issue I want to work through, forming a clear image of it in my head, including how it affects me and how it would make me feel to overcome it.

Step 4: Headphones on. Press play.

Step 5: Feel the beat and breathe deeply as it fills my head. Immerse myself in the music and lyrics. Don't let myself be distracted by voices or outside impressions. Even as I'm listening, I look forward to hearing it again.

Step 6: Start doing something else – write, doodle, surf the web, whatever. As long as it's solitary and focused – no messaging or playing games – and doesn't disrupt the peace I'm trying to find. This step can also work when I'm on a treadmill or going for a walk. I keep my eyes fixed on the horizon and walk with purpose, which increases feelings of confidence and gives me a boost. My favourite thing to do – surprise, surprise! – is write whatever comes to mind, even if it's nonsense – but not on a treadmill, obviously!

Step 7: When I listen to a song on repeat while thinking deeply about an issue, I soon realize how far I've come in my thought process. The repetition reminds me of where I started and how far I have come in resolving the issue in my head. Association is a powerful tool.

WRITING:

I write all the time. I need to write as much as I need to breathe. A lot of what I write is therapy for me, for my eyes only, and other times it turns into a blog post or book! So, here's a tip for using writing as a tool in recovery:

Just write. Whatever comes to mind. Unfiltered, unedited. Trust the process. Even if it doesn't make sense or you're just slinging out random words. Freewriting, writing without any plan or thought to the words, can be liberating, although I always correct my spelling along the way – #nerd. Write for as long as you need and, once you're done, leave it. Save the document, put your notebook aside, go on the internet or do something else for a while. Then, when you feel ready to return to your writing, read it through and pay attention to how it makes you feel.

As with playing a song on repeat while working through an issue, I can look at what I have written and say, "Ah, I felt like this five minutes ago, I'm seeing it in a different light now," which can provide relief and comfort. Or, if I'm still feeling grotty, at least I now have something tangible to work with next time I see my psychiatrist. Instead of sitting there going "Um… uh…" and having nothing to say, I have some material I can use in my meeting with him. It's up to you whether you share your thoughts word for word or simply use it as inspiration. I find that I just glance over my notes and maybe share just 30 per cent of what I have written. However, every part of my writing counts and, even though I might only share a little of it, the other 70 per cent has not been for nothing.

Alternatively, if you're feeling a bit worried, you can write an email to your psychiatrist right away, but I would advise you to sleep on it. I find that the crazed ramblings I might produce at 3am don't necessarily apply when I wake up the following morning! And then I have the added stress of mild embarrassment and awkwardness trying to explain why I pressed send on something I've actually already processed in my mind and moved on from.

EPILOGUE

All's well that ends well, right?

I think it is important to emphasize that, although it might seem as if my recovery has been a breeze, it hasn't. I am a naturally positive person with a strong support network, and I follow my doctors' advice, but it has required an inordinate amount of willpower and determination to get where I am today. I still have many things that I struggle with in daily life.

Schizophrenia is not pretty. I would go so far as to say that it's an ugly illness. From the chaotic and confusing breakdown, through the rocky stages of recovery and all the strange behaviour, anger outbursts and awkward communication that entails, it takes an exceptional disposition to cope with the mayhem caused by the disease. This applies to both sufferers and their families and carers. One goes from being a perfectly normal, well-balanced person to requiring help with making conversation and carrying out basic daily tasks. Someone who used to be able to juggle school, homework, after-school activities, a job and a social life suddenly finds themselves incapacitated, unable to string two words together or stay focused on anything for more than five minutes. You may find that people you thought were your friends suddenly distance themselves from you. Unfortunately, not everyone is equipped to deal with mental illness, so it's easier to just steer clear than ask you how you're doing. Of course, all of this is devastating – a huge blow to one's self-confidence and shocking for everyone involved. As you emerge from your psychosis, you might feel mortified about some of the things you said and did when you were at your most psychotic. This is perfectly natural but, when you start to get better again, things will take on a clearer perspective. It is important to understand that your behaviour while psychotic is not your fault. You were controlled by a ghastly illness that attacks your brain – it wasn't you deciding what your actions should be, it was the schizophrenia. I hope this relieves some of the guilt or shame you might be feeling. I still struggle with embarrassment sometimes, but I remind myself that I was unwell, not deliberately setting out to hurt people and self-destruct in the process.

As mentioned before, people in the throes of psychosis aren't known for their self-awareness, as we're too busy fighting voices, paranoia and ambivalence to see ourselves from the outside. Something I noticed during my recovery is how difficult seemingly simple tasks became. For many years, I couldn't leave the house on my own – my poor mum would have to take me to the pharmacy, accompany me to doctor and dental appointments, sit with me at the hairdresser, join me to shop for essentials, etc. I never went shopping alone – I initially found this too overwhelming. There were too many stresses, such as being approached by shop assistants, feeling observed (paranoia alert), the panic of being in a changing room with a long queue waiting outside, feeling pressured to make small talk with the cashier when it didn't come naturally, and the over-stimulation of walking into a shop full of colours, lights, sounds, patterns and textures that would bring me to a grinding halt in the middle of the aisle. There were so many choices that I didn't know where to start.

I am now able to go shopping more easily – Mum says, "Too easily!" – as long as I am prepared and calm. That means I have my purse, my phone, my water bottle, my Akineton (anti-side effects medication) and every other necessity with me, and my outfit is clean.

* * *

Writing is my therapy, and not a day goes by without me typing or using my favourite pen and notebooks. I write to cope. I write to feel alive. I write to communicate. Compiling this book has been very helpful for me and I hope that it benefits you too. Please feel free to leave a book review or follow me via my social media handles, which you'll find at the end of the book, to see more of my journey through schizophrenia.

Thank you for choosing this book – I really appreciate it.

SOCIAL MEDIA

WRITER PROFILE
Facebook – Georgia's Voice (there are two pages with this name –
here's the link to mine: https://www.facebook.com/georgiasvoice)
Instagram – @georgiasvoices
Twitter – @GeorgiaBrask

ARTIST PROFILE
Facebook – Art by Georgia Brask
Instagram – @artbygeorgiabrask

MOUSE PROFILE
Facebook – Mr Mouse Design
Instagram – @mrmousedesign

BLOG
https://georgiasvoices.blogspot.com

WEBSITE
https://georgiabrask.dk

ACKNOWLEDGEMENTS

Thanks to...

My strong, funny and endlessly patient family, with a special mention for my fantastic Farfar.

My amazing friends mentioned in the book.

My *Gulddyssen* ceramics group.

Incredible Helle and everyone at Bisque.

Lovely Birgit who sews beautiful things for me and has been such a support to me.

My doctor Niels Ulrich and all the medical and psychiatric professionals who have helped and supported me throughout.

The incredibly kind and lovely new friends I have made during this journey.

ABOUT CHERISH EDITIONS

Cherish Editions is a bespoke author-funded publishing service for mental health, well-being and inspirational books.

As a division of the TriggerHub Group, the UK's leading independent mental health and well-being organization, we are experienced in creating and selling positive, responsible, important and inspirational pieces of bibliotherapy. Our books harness the power of a person's lived experience to guide others through their own mental health journeys and kick-start their recovery. We also work to de-stigmatize the issues around mental health and improve the well-being of those who read our titles.

Founded by Adam Shaw, a mental health advocate, author and philanthropist, and leading psychologist Lauren Callaghan, Cherish Editions aims to publish books that provide advice, support and inspiration. We nurture our authors so that their stories can unfurl on the page, helping them to share their uplifting and moving stories.

Cherish Editions is unique in that a percentage of the profits from the sale of our books goes directly to leading mental health charity Shawmind, to deliver its vision to provide support for those experiencing mental ill health.

Find out more about Cherish Editions by visiting cherisheditions.com or by joining us on:
Twitter @cherisheditions
Facebook @cherisheditions
Instagram @cherisheditions

Cherish
EDITIONS

ABOUT SHAWMIND

A proportion of profits from the sale of all Trigger books go to their sister charity, Shawmind, also founded by Adam Shaw and Lauren Callaghan. The charity aims to ensure that everyone has access to mental health resources whenever they need them. You can find out more about the work Shawmind do by visiting shawmind.org or joining them on:

Twitter @Shawmind_
Facebook @ShawmindUK
Instagram @Shawmind_

Lightning Source UK Ltd.
Milton Keynes UK
UKHW041235170123
415491UK00004B/73

9 781913 615680